The Gucci Gang Story

Julia Thomas

Dedication

This book is dedicated to my true love, the love of my life, Steven Daniel Harrod. He tragically passed away on May 6th, 2024. Our love story and how we met was an inspiration to write this book.

Acknowledgment

I want to thank my family, most of all, my brother Hendry Muljadi and his wife Ashley Muljadi, who have been my support system. They have helped me through so much since Steven's passing.

My best friends Andrea O'Berry, Faylan Harvey, See Thongsouk, Eric Orcutt, my daughter Payton Wilson, and the church family at Lutheran of Hope.

I want to acknowledge several people who helped me put this book together, starting with Steven's kids, who played a part in my life to make this story come to life.

I want to thank my best friend, Andrea O'Berry, and my sister-in-law, Ashley Muljadi, for reading my manuscript and taking great photos.

Most of all, I want to thank my daughter Payton Wilson who inspires me every day to be a better person and mom. I would like to thank God, our Lord, for giving me the inspiration to write this story that came to me in my dreams—from the first day I met Steven and the subsequent days until he died. The Lord's message was very clear: I was meant to write this story about the journey I have endured since childhood to meet Steven, how we fell in love at first sight, and the tragic story of how he died. Every step of the way and every word I have written was blessed in the name of Jesus. God inspired me to write this book, and through it all, it helped me heal throughout this journey of grief.

About the Author

Julia Thomas came to the USA as an immigrant on January 1, 1988. She is of Chinese descent but was born and raised in Indonesia until she was ten years old. Learning the English language was a struggle at first, but after a few months, she picked it up rather quickly. She moved around a lot due to her parents' inability in finding work.

Julia's journey started in Los Angeles, where she stayed with family and friends for just a few months until the money ran out. She and her family then moved to Sioux City, Iowa, so that her father could find work in the trucking business as a driver for a local Asian trucking company. After just eight months, the family had bigger dreams and took the risk to move back to California. This time, they settled in San Francisco.

Her family flourished in the Bay Area, maintaining stable work in the catering business that led them to serve over 100 customers a day. But despite their savings, they still couldn't afford the house of their dreams in the California housing market. Taking another risk, they moved back to the

Midwest—this time to Ames, Iowa, where housing was much more affordable. They had money left over to start the restaurant business they had always dreamed of.

In August 1992, they opened their Indonesian-Chinese restaurant. The business was a success and fed all Julia's siblings—two brothers—in their family of five. The American dream of success finally came true, but it wasn't always easy.

Being an immigrant daughter wasn't all roses and petals. She had to work hard from the age of 10 in the catering industry in San Francisco, and the work got even harder when the restaurant opened. Her parents' rule was: if you want a roof over your head and food in your belly, you work every waking hour dedicated to the restaurant, except during school hours. After school, her day consisted only of making egg rolls and crab rangoons, sweeping, mopping, slicing, dicing, and a few other tasks while doing her homework and still maintaining good grades. There was no such thing as fun until work was done, and she worked 12 hours on weekends.

She had disagreements with her dad growing up that made her feel like she never had a positive male role model. She made many wrong choices in choosing men as partners and had been married and divorced more than twice. At the age of 46, Julia finally met her soulmate. They fell in love at first sight on February 2, 2024, when she and Steve met each other. Their love was magical, rare, and unique like no other love story ever told before. Tragically, after only 90 days together, she lost the love of her life to death.

Contents

Chapter 1: NF

Where were you, NF, when I was 11? Your music would have been a godsend. Instead, the only faith music on the radio was Amy Grant. No disrespect to her, but how's a kid from the hood supposed to relate? Blasting Amy Grant on my Walkman would've gotten me beat up daily getting off the bus. Jesus, let's get real here.

Living in the hood, trying to fit in with the Black, Mexican, and even Asian kids... I'd look in the mirror, and I would only see Asians. I had no choice but to be hard as an Asian. Fitting in with any group was nearly impossible and confusing at eleven. Daily struggles to find my place were almost impossible. I tried different crowds, each attempt at a new adventure and identity.

My first group was the Black girls at Roosevelt Middle School in San Francisco. I mimicked their speech, style, and attitude. I even had the soul sister trench coat with old-school black and white Nikes. I looked sweet, with my hard-ass look to match. I acted tough, talked tough, dressed tough -

everything, but my skin color did not match. And that was the one thing I couldn't change.

But no matter how tough I acted or how cold and fearless I appeared, the world never feared me enough to leave me alone. Twice a week, they'd catch me at 26th and Mission. At eleven, I was defending my identity against people full of hate who didn't understand my pain. Physical and verbal fights were common, and I contributed once or twice. I was fearless, throwing punches to defend my skinny little ass. I came out swinging, even against the tall white girl who claimed to be Italian – Janis Ajello.

Janis Ajello - there's a name I haven't thought about in years. She was one of only two white girls in our school at the time. The other one, her cousin, I can't even remember her name. She must not have been on my radar. But Janis, for a brief month, became my friend. We bonded over New Kids on the Block. That girl was obsessed, and she made me obsessed, too. *"Hangin' Tough"* took over my brain. Suddenly, I had my first boy band crush. Good God, that was a difficult time. Joey McIntyre and Jonathan Knight - I liked those curly blonde boys. Joey was my first love.

After that phase fizzled out, I hung out with the Mexican kids. Melissa Trujillo stands out - tough as nails with her hair always in a bun. She looked like someone's mom at eleven! But she had a good side I admired. Melissa showed me how to wear eyeliner dramatically and burn Maybelline pencils with a lighter. She rocked bright red or dark red lipstick daily and even smoked cigarettes. I thought she was cool, but God helped me say no to the smoke. I didn't think God would find that cool.

Melissa and I became real friends. For the first time, I felt accepted at this school. She showed me a world I hadn't known before - one of bold makeup and even bolder attitudes. But, like all things at that age, our friendship eventually fizzled. Next on the friendship train was Dana Tran, my second bestie. She was good, a bit nerdy, but super sweet and smart as a whip. Always sick with a cold, that girl. She lived up to the *"smart Asian girl"* stereotype that my parents wanted me to be. I couldn't keep up with her intellectually, but we formed a bond that gave me peace for the second time in my young life.

This friendship with Dana came after the loss of Mary Salazar, my first real childhood friend, in 5th grade. Mary lived in apartment 8, and we were in apartment 6. We'd play in the hallway between our homes, best friends throughout 5th grade. Then, a drunk driver took her life at Vallejo Mall, her body torn apart and spread over 300 yards from the mall entrance. Her mom gave me Mary's clothes after she died. I kept her alive in my memory as long as I could, dreaming of her every night for six months, unable to let go.

Losing Mary was my first real encounter with loss. It shattered my young heart, crumbling my world for the first time. This devastating loss turned me to God at eleven. I had no one else to turn to. Through my journey of healing, I found solace in faith, speaking to God every day since.

Fast forward to June 1992, after a couple of years of friendship with Dana. The news hit: we were moving to Iowa. Where the heck was Iowa? Did they grow potatoes there? My world shattered all over again. Holy moly, someone tip the cow, please!

The summer of ‘92 was my year. Everything changed. I lived, laughed, danced, and cried with friends, new and old. I pushed boundaries like never before, and I was no longer my father’s obedient Asian daughter. I was reborn, caring little about what anyone thought - not my parents, not anyone. I became my own person, living in the moment without regrets or consequences.

That summer, I met people who shaped my life. My experiences in the summer of ‘92 molded me into the person I am today. I had my first crush on an Asian boy – Ngai Pham. Now, I’m not laughing because Asian boys are funny. On the contrary, most I’ve met aren’t funny at all. Very boring, in fact. Not trying to be biased or negative here; not all Asian boys are the same. But this guy, he was different. Cool, dreamy, with that hair and the ponytail. He wore MC Hammer pants. That was my jam.

We met on 4 July, stranded on the Golden Gate Bridge after I snuck out to a party. There was no ride or way of getting home, and I knew I’d get whooped when I got back. But I didn’t care. Face the consequences later, after the fun.

The day before we left for Iowa, I ran away. Thought I was being clever. My dad didn't find it as amusing as I did. I eventually came home and got beaten with a water hose, but every scar was worth it. The heavy water hose hitting my back and legs felt like nothing compared to the pain hovering in my head. The real pain was feeling unloved by my earthly father. He couldn't see my struggles or pain, maybe too caught up in his own. At the time, I didn't understand. I hated my father to the core and my mother even more for never protecting me from his wrath. My grandparents from the Machari side were visiting that year. I eavesdropped and heard my grandfather telling my father that I needed to be disciplined and punished in the strongest possible way. *"Don't be afraid to punish her,"* he said, *"because if it doesn't start now, that girl will be pregnant and knocked up tomorrow."* My grandmother chimed in, telling my father to teach my mother a lesson, too. *"Make sure she gets in line and does what you say. She's a shitty wife who can't cook right."* This was the Machari family's hate toward my mother. I'd seen it since I was three years old and experienced it in the front row. My older brother, Hunter Machari, didn't see it in depth, and my younger brother, Philip Machari, was too young to know. I was the buffer between both families.

On 1st August 1992, we hit the road for Ankeny, IA. I was literally sick to my stomach, vomiting again due to anxiety.

Looking back, I'm grateful for the aunts who loved me as a child - Lintang Lia Machari, Citra Machari, and Raini Machari. Raini passed away about ten years ago, only 50 years old. I adored her very much. I had many sleepovers at my grandparents' house in the Philippines, and those are some of my happiest childhood memories of the Machari family.

My first memory of Grandpa Machari was special. He taught me work ethic before anyone else did. The man showed me how to wash the entire family's dishes by hand. In the early '80s in the Philippines, we were very poor. Dishwashers were unheard of. I enjoyed the lesson, though I didn't understand its value until much later. Both my Machari grandparents are gone now, and I miss them very much. At the time, I didn't give them the grace they deserved. I have never felt true love from my Machari grandparents. I suppressed all these good memories I had with my Machari family and only kept the good memories of my mom's side of the family.

My mother's family is Ouyang. I was brainwashed only to remember good Ouyang family memories. The Ouyang family is better, I was told. Pure and honest and good. The Machari family was portrayed as evil and mean, like the devil. My mother and her entire family programmed this into my head my entire life.

The Ouyang family is one tight-knit group. They do cover-ups very well. Heck, I guess both families did. They're all about keeping up appearances and never tarnishing the family name. We were taught never to speak what's in our hearts, always to be ashamed, and never to make mistakes. It was considered a sin to talk about anything real. Gossip was the Ouyang family's special trait. The gossip was always about the Machari family and the neighbors in town.

This was all I knew until I went through intensive therapy to uncover all my memories when I was 40 years old, during my marriage to Dennis Tyler. It wasn't until these deep reconditioning therapy sessions that I realized the Machari family wasn't the enemy my mother had made them out to be. I unlocked suppressed memories and saw both families in a new light. Looking back at that summer of '92, I realize now how pivotal it was. It was the last gasp of my childhood, the moment I started to become my own person. I never asked for permission again after that. I only acted and lived in the moment, consequences be damned.

The move to Iowa felt like the end of the world then, but it was really the beginning of a new chapter. I left behind the complexity of trying to fit in with different ethnic groups in San Francisco, only to face new challenges in the Midwest. But that's a story for another chapter.

As I write this now, I can't help but wonder: if NF had been around when I was eleven, would things have been different? Would his music have given me the words to express my feelings and the strength to face my challenges head-on? Maybe. But then again, maybe those struggles were exactly what I needed to become who I am today.

In the end, it was God who saw me through those turbulent years. From the moment I turned to Him at eleven, reeling from the loss of Mary, He's been my constant companion. Through the beatings, the confusion, the attempts to fit in, and the eventual realization that I needed to be true to myself - God was there.

And now, as I look back on that little girl trying so hard to be tough, to be accepted, to understand her place in the world, I feel a deep compassion. If I could, I'd go back and tell her: *"You're stronger than you know. Your struggles will shape you, but they won't break you. Keep talking to God. Keep pushing forward. One day, you'll understand it all and be thankful for every step of the journey."* But I can't do that, so I'll do the next best thing. I'll share my story, hoping that somewhere out there, another kid struggling to fit in and understand their place in the world might find some comfort, inspiration, and hope. Because in the end, that's what it's all about - finding our way through the chaos, holding onto faith, and becoming the people we're meant to be.

Chapter 2: Days After You Left

The days after you left were a blur of pain, regret, and overwhelming grief. I'm so sorry I didn't listen to what you were trying to tell me in those last three months. Now that you're gone, I finally understand, but it's too late. I should have fought harder for you and been more insistent about your drinking. I should have stopped you from leaving in frustration that Saturday. I should have been more patient and kept fighting for us like I always did when you had doubts. I'm sorry I didn't stop you from leaving that night. If I had, you'd still be here with me, Teagan, Carter, and Bailey. I got scared because I've been through this before and didn't want to push you to the edge. I didn't realize how deep into the ocean you had already swum.

You were the love of my life, even though we were only together for a few months. You showed me how I deserved to love myself, and I only wanted you to love yourself the way God loves you. Every day since you came into my life, I laughed harder and smiled more than ever before. You brought so much joy in the short time I knew you.

God placed you in my life at the right time when we needed each other, and we did have the fairytale ending that we always talked about. You meant every word when you said you would never give up on us but would die trying. I know you did what you had to do to find your peace with God. I know you're happy and finally at peace, exactly where you want to be. It took a while for me to come to terms with the fact that you were gone. You can finally rest your head, dance, and sing all the songs you used to sing to me in heaven. I'll catch you in my dreams, babe. Dream sweet, my sweet man. I don't know how to put one foot in front of the other now that you're gone. I feel blessed and loved by my friends and family.

We once promised that if one of us were not here, we would be the missing parent. You were a man with so much love to give, and you gave me the best love, the kind of love that Jesus wants for all of us. We sure loved each other like nothing else existed. We had plans we talked about until one of us went. We were going to get married after one month, but Avery said to wait 12 months of the season. We haven't even reached summer yet. I will continue with those plans we made, and I will love your boys the way you loved them. Rest in peace, my perfect man.

The night I accepted your passing, I did everything to remember you. I busted out Ritz crackers and chocolate milk. I will never say goodbye to you, Sutton Harrington. I say I will see you soon. I'm coming, and we'll have that eternal love like we said we would. When we were shopping for your new shades just browsing around, we should've picked up those shades you really liked, but you wouldn't allow me to buy them for you. We were truly happy and blessed to have the kind of love we shared that only we and God know. I remember the night prior to your passing on May 5, at 3:45 PM, you left this song *"Misery Avenue"* by Juice WRLD. I'm home, staring at the hot tub, wanting to be close to you and look at the stars like we did. It's undergoing some work right now. I want to be near you so I can feel you next to me. I don't want to forget the smell of your skin. A few days after your passing, I went to Chapel Hill Cemetery to visit Grandma Barbara and your place of final resting peace. I tied your traveling toothbrush to Grandma's marker. I didn't want you to be without your toothbrush. You know how I got on you about brushing your teeth every night before you doze off on the couch?

After two weeks of heavy grieving that included denial, blaming, hating you, and crying for hours, my friend Summer messaged me and invited me over to her place. We sat and talked about her life, and I realized that I am blessed to have had the love that we shared, and it was time for me to stop crying. Have you ever cried so much that you shed blood tears? I saw myself in the mirror, and I saw the side of my eyes was so chapped that it created a cut and bled. This is when I knew I needed to get myself together for the kids. A few days later, she invited me to the Willie Nelson Concert at Common's Lake Park. It was a blast. That was the first day that I smiled since you left us. The concert was outside with beautiful, perfect weather. I wish you were here; you would've had a blast. We talked about going to concerts and events together. You were with me in spirit.

At the end of May, I finally got to meet your oldest son, Jacob Clark, and your grandson, Caleb.

We all drove to Waukee and spent the whole day with them. He looks so much like you and has the same fears and demons as you. I know you talked about him a lot when you were still alive. I've wanted to meet him since the first day I met you. At that time, you were still heavily dealing with your demons, and I wanted to give you the time you needed. I guess we never got around to doing that. I reached out to him on Facebook shortly after your passing. I am so glad I got to meet him, and he's now part of my family. My family has grown from Piper and me to Teagan, Carter, Ava, Casey, Jacob, Ashley, Bailey, and Caleb. My Sam's card really comes in useful now.

I've been through lots of bad relationships in my 46 years, marriages, divorces and lost loved ones. I thought I found my person a couple of times but had the rug pulled out from under me. I never stayed in a relationship that I didn't see value or respect in. I never settled, and I have extremely high standards. Most of my friends can attest to that. Before you, I had my running shoes on all the time. I ran from relationships when they got too real because I was afraid to get broken again. When you and I met, it was magical for us; the little red flags didn't seem to matter to me. I didn't run like I normally would. You made me stay. You made me put my running shoes away. I never settled; no one should settle for less than their worth. You will find your person no matter how long it takes. I found you, Sutton, at the right time. It was God's plan.

Tonight, I am sitting here watching the Bart Story from MercyMe. I'm sorry that we didn't get the chance to watch this. We talked for hours about it and listened to this song. I will continue to tell your story even if no one is reading. I will document every memory that I have as my mind will soon wither away, and all I have are these documents to tell your story and our story. It will be a blessing when my mind soon fades; I will no longer be in pain. Just like I told you, but God had other plans for you. He left me behind so He could heal me.

When I start losing my memory, you're not going to be there to remind me. I will continue to document and believe what I read when my memory is gone. As we talked about, we have our story, and I will only remember for a short time before everything fades away.

On May 12, 2024, I'm here for Mother's Day service at Valley Church. I saved you a seat in the upper level on the right, second row, seats 4 and 5. I know you're with me. I can feel you holding my hand. I will continue the Saturday night service like we planned until I see you again. I miss you every moment of every day. A few days later, we grilled burgers, and the boys played pickleball, and basketball, all of us together, and saved you a seat. I'm sure you would've still kicked Teagan's ass in basketball. Your family – all of us, Teagan, Carter, Ava, Casey, Bailey, and Piper – shared memories of you, which filled all our hearts. Carter played a few songs on his guitar like I've always wanted. We will have more nights like tonight, like we planned. God has all of us, Sutton Harrington. On May 16, 2024, I was feeling lonely and missing you. I tried on your recently acquired Nike shoes. Dang, babe, you got some giant ass feet, good Lord. I think both my feet can fit in one. I barely wear a size 6 in women's, and you wear 13 in men's. On May 19, 2024, at Valley Church, I tried to have all the kids come with me to the service, but unfortunately, I failed. Just you and me... They will show up soon. It'll be like we dreamed of.

Today is the day. Piper's Graduation at Xtream Arena. I saved you a seat; her graduation party was on June 18, 2024. We had been planning this for months, babe... Took 6 hours to execute... I had a lot of help from all the boys to get this party going. Wish you were here. I know you're here in spirit.

I've been battling mental illness for over 35 years. My illness flared up in April. Today is the first day since then, especially since you've been gone, so I feel a bit more normal. With the help of many doctors through all this, I am able to be up at 5:30 am this morning. I had a coffee, worked out, had breakfast, and could sit and write my book this morning, plus have a morning swim.

Today is the start of a new beginning of healing... I document my stories, am real to myself, and am honest with myself when no one is looking. Only GOD can see you. Jesus, my savior, heard my cries at eleven. *"Boys Don't Cry"* by Jake Banfield – I was told never to cry when I got beaten as a child. Not only boys were told not to cry. I feel this sense of sadness come over me again. I guess grief goes through many stages that I wasn't prepared for. I find myself sitting in front of the long mirror that I have next to my side of the bed, saying these words:

I will stand in your presence.

I will stand in your glory.

I will fall to my knees.

I will dance with you, Jesus.

Jesus, please ask our Heavenly Father if there is a place in heaven that has my name on it. I've lived a full life. I've experienced many journeys, been to many places, and seen many things.

I've loved, hurt, suffered, and healed.

In Jesus' name, I pray. Amen

As I sit here, reflecting on all that has happened, I can't help but feel a mix of emotions. The pain of losing you is still raw, but there's also a sense of gratitude for the love we shared, no matter how brief. You taught me so much about love, about myself, and about life. Even in your absence, you continue to shape my world.

I look around the home – our home – and see traces of you everywhere. The coffee mug you always used sits on the kitchen counter. Your favorite chair in the living room seems to hold the imprint of your body. The garden we started together is blooming now, a testament to the life and love we nurtured.

I'm trying to keep my promise to you to be there for your boys. It's not easy, but it's a labor of love. They remind me so much of you – Teagan's laugh, Carter's thoughtful gaze, Bailey's mischievous smile. Through them, a part of you lives on, and I'm grateful for that. Some days are harder than others. There are moments when the weight of your absence feels crushing, and I struggle to breathe. But then I remember your strength, your resilience, and I find the courage to face another day. I'll talk to you, you know. I like to think you can hear me in the quiet moments of the night or when I'm driving alone in the car.

I'm learning to navigate this new reality, this life without you physically in it. It's a journey I never wanted to take, but one I'm facing with as much grace as I can muster. I'm trying to honor your memory by living fully, loving deeply, and being the person you always saw in me.

Your passing has made me reflect on my own journey, my battles with mental health, my relationships, my faith. I'm working on healing, growing, and becoming stronger. It's what you would have wanted for me, I think.

As I end this chapter, I want you to know that you are loved, you are missed, and you will never be forgotten. Your impact on my life, on the lives of your children, and on all those who knew you are indelible. You may have left this earthly plane, but your spirit lives on in our hearts and memories.

Until we meet again, my love, keep a seat warm for me up there, okay? And know that down here, I'm doing my best to live a life that would make you proud. Your love continues to guide me, inspire me, and comfort me. In that way, you're still here, still with me, every step of the way. Rest in peace, my sweet Sutton. I love you, always and forever.

Chapter 3: Music of Grief

It's been nearly a month since you left, and I miss you like crazy. The silence in our home is deafening, broken only by the occasional strains of *"Twin Flame"* by Machine Gun Kelly. I play it every night, imagining your happy face singing it to me. It was our song, wasn't it? The one that spoke of a love so intense, so immediate, that it felt like we'd known each other in a past life.

Falling asleep and waking up in your arms every morning was a gift I'll carry with me until I join you in God's kingdom. We laughed, we danced, we dreamed, and we cried together. Now, I'm left with the ghost of your embrace, a hollow echo of the warmth we shared. We always said we didn't know what love was until we met. How could we have known that one day would feel like a month, a week like a year, and a month like five years?

I understand now that it was God's gift to us because He had other plans for you, my love. He needed an angel in Heaven, and He chose you. Our paths crossed, and the life-altering experience we shared was all part of His grand design. That's why it always felt like we knew each other from a past life. We used to talk about how our paths could have crossed in 2005, but that wasn't God's plan. The plan was for us to meet at the exact time we did, to share a love so profound that it would last an eternity, even if our time together were cut short. I've weathered many storms in my lifetime, and so have you. We met at the perfect time, healing each other's past brokenness and making a promise never to give up. I listen to our song every night since you've been gone, imagining your radiant face as you sang it. By the way, I found that cute handwritten note you left me on 4/15/24 a couple of days ago. *"Love you more from the five great oceans to the one hundred thirteen seas,"* you wrote. Oh, how those words make my heart race and ache at the same time.

Remember that TikTok video, *"Motivated by His Grace"?* We made that promise to each other that night. We always worked through our challenges and came out stronger than before. We vowed never to give up or die trying. Now, you're gone, yet I can still feel you all around me as if you never left. I keep replaying all our conversations, plans and promises – from the type of beach chair we'd have when we retired in Tulum, Mexico, to all the places we dreamed of visiting together.

I want you to know that we're still going to take those trips, and you're coming with us. You'll see, laugh, and cry with us through the rest of our life journey. The best part? You get to fly for free now. You would've been smiling ear to ear and be the proudest grandpa – Bailey went on about ten rides, including a roller coaster, and didn't even cry. He was such a stud. I took all the kids on an adventure. His birthday is coming up, and we're taking him to Disney so he can ride the big kid rides.

Every day, I pray for a breakthrough, especially since you left us. Part of me still doesn't want to accept that you're gone. I can feel your spirit with me every day, and I wonder if this feeling will ever end. The pain inside me is overwhelming, and I don't know how much longer I can hold on.

I know God is always in my heart, and everything is in His name. I know He is capable of all things and can make miracles happen. I pray for you to come home where you belong, but my faith is shaken, and my mind wanders to dark places. I can't seem to grasp reality. I know this is real, but I pinch myself daily to ensure it's not just a bad dream. The thoughts going through my head scare me, and being far from you terrifies me.

The day after you left, I broke down on my hands and knees, begging God that this wasn't real. Our last words to each other weren't pleasant. We argued the last time I saw you. I replay that night in my head over and over, wishing I had done something different. I didn't fight for you like I should have. I didn't physically stop you from leaving when you were upset. I should have done everything in my power to keep you with me.

You texted right away after you left, but I didn't respond until 12 hours later in the morning. You left me with so many clues that I didn't understand. It was your cry for help, and I didn't get to you soon enough to rescue you. I failed to decipher the songs and messages you left that had hidden meanings. If only I had reached you sooner when you sent those songs. All these *"what ifs"* are darkening my mind and shaking my faith. I wonder why God placed you in my life only to take you away when your healing journey started. I've lost so many people in my life

– my best friend Mary, other friends, my previous partner Dennis, and now you. I could handle anything, but I feel defeated and lost in God's love right now.

I know God doesn't give me more than I can handle. I know I am strong, and I am not alone. But it doesn't make losing you any easier. I pray for a miracle to help us all honor and remember you as the loving father and soulmate that you were. I'm afraid I'm losing this battle. It's getting harder and harder for me to see hope. With every step I take, I feel knocked down. Every accomplishment is met with another obstacle. I feel defeated.

Music has always been our sanctuary, hasn't it? I remember the first time I saw your picture, I thought you were Eminem's twin. I never told you that – maybe I did in my sleep. You always said you were going to record me talking in my sleep. I didn't want your head to get too big if I told you that you looked like Eminem's twin. We couldn't have that. If we were both big-headed, someone needed to stay humble. I stayed humble so you could shine.

Songs like *"I'm Not Alone"* by Kari Jobe have gotten me through so much. It has healed my heart and made me feel safe and not alone. I know that God is always with me, no matter what obstacles are in my way. I pray this song will be healing for me once again.

Remember how excited we were when we found out Dax made it to Christian music? We'll all still see him at the fair on August 10, 2024, as planned. You'll be there with us in spirit; I know it. If you ever had the opportunity to watch the story of Bart Millard from MercyMe, you'd see how similar our journeys have been. Like Bart, I found God when I was young, feeling helpless, scared, lost, and unloved. God has been my Heavenly Father since I was eleven. My life journey has been a long walk with God by my side. I've been through more trauma than five people combined, but I'm strong because I have my Heavenly Father walking beside me every step of the way. I've survived when any normal person would crumble. God will never forsake me.

I understand now why you left me songs like *"Don't Let Go"* and *"Play This When I'm Gone"* by MGK. They were clues you left for me to find you, messages I didn't comprehend until it was too late. You always left me clues and messages from the beginning. I told you I wouldn't let you go, and you got scared. I remember how you sang *"Bloody Valentine"* to me on February 15th after that Valentine's Day fiasco, with the most sincere, heartfelt apology.

I've stopped asking questions about why you left me and the boys. I'll chalk it up to God needing you more right now in heaven. I've stopped seeking answers I'll never get until I meet my Maker. I will trust in God's plan, in His mercy, grace, and love, to get us all through the loss of you. You will always be my white cheddar, and I will always be your Tia C. A wise friend gave me the song *"We Are Gonna Be Ok"* by Brian & Jenn Johnson. It's gotten me through the loss of Piper's dad, and I've listened to it over a thousand times since you left. We need to say what we mean in our hearts to the people we love with kindness, compassion, and utmost understanding. We need to look at each other not as enemies but as a family; we're all struggling with pain and grief.

We mourn in our own ways – there is no right or wrong way to grieve as long as we're true to our hearts and to God. All sorts of emotions going in different directions make navigating difficult and almost impossible. Together, we can be more understanding of each other's moods. Not everyone can be happy and smiling during these times. We need to show love and kindness when we see our loved ones struggle in their moments of sadness.

Most importantly, we need to extend more forgiveness toward the people we love and others. It's the only way to heal ourselves. You'd be surprised by how clear your mind and soul can become and how much lighter your heart will feel. This way, we can accept God as our savior and let Him take all our burdens, pains, and worries.

We will heal, we will rise, and we will rejoice again in Jesus' name. Amen.

Chapter 4: First Date

Ninety days and nights, we bared our souls to each other. Laughter, tears, and everything in between. I can't forget taking you to church that first time - they were handing out palm leaves for some special occasion I can't remember to save my life. You got all creative, turning that palm into a ring. The next thing I know, we're having a naked kitchen wedding, with counters cluttered with everything but the kitchen sink. All that yakking for three months straight, it was like we were gearing up for the next quarter till I'd see you again. This is the stuff I'd been dreaming about, day in and day out. If God took me now, I'd go peacefully. When my memory's shot, it'll be pure bliss.

It all kicked off when you swiped right on that Facebook dating app. I clicked on your profile, and boom - there you were. Now, I'll be honest, bald guys aren't usually my type, but damn if you didn't look fine. Then I spotted you were Jill Logan's buddies, which sealed the deal. I didn't beat around the bush; I just asked if you were free on 2/4/2024 to meet up at Vista Pub in the west part of Iowa City at 1 pm that Sunday. You hit me back right away with a big fat yes. On the day off, I was running behind with errands, so I had to push it to 2 pm at Hu Hot instead. You were cool as a cucumber about it.

I rolled up a minute late, hustling through that heavy door. There you were, looking nervous as hell but sporting the sweetest smile I'd ever seen. Felt like some higher power gave me a shove right into your space. The hostess got us seated, and that's when things got interesting.

"Is your name really Joslyn?" you asked, all serious-like.

I couldn't help but chuckle. *"Yeah, why's that?"*

"Oh, nothing," you said, trying to play it cool.

In my head, I'm thinking, *"Jesus, what a weirdo."* But something kept me glued to my seat, curiosity getting better.

I couldn't let it slide after we grabbed our food at the grill. *"So, what's the deal with asking if Joslyn is my real name?"*

You started sweating like a pig at a barbecue - a cute pig, but still. *"Where do I even start?"*

"Beginning's usually a good place," I shot back, giving you my best 'spill it' look.

That's when you unloaded about your J curse. Josephine, heartbreak numero uno. June, the sequel. Jordan, the trilogy. I must've looked like I'd been smacked with a frying pan 'cause you started backpedaling faster than a crawfish in a pot.

"Guess I never learn," you said, looking like you wanted to melt into the floor.

I couldn't help but laugh. *"Alright, you've got my attention. Let's hear it."*

As you spilled your guts, I realized not all your J's were bad news. There was Jill Logan Martinez, someone I knew from a long time ago. Small world, right? That connection was like the Man Upstairs giving us a nudge.

"Hold up," I said, feeling a bit defensive of my name. *"Not all J's are out to get you. I get Josephine, June, and Jordan. But Jill is a good egg. Then there's me, Joslyn, and I'm not about to hurt you. And let's not forget Jesus - He's not going anywhere."*

You flashed this dorky but adorable smile and reached for my hand. *"Thanks,"* you said, and something just clicked.

But me being me, I had to go and stick my foot in it. *"You know, I've never been into bald guys. Never thought I'd fall for one. Good Lord... This is weird... you're as bald as they come! First time for everything, I guess... Snoop Doggy Dog."* My favorite statement to say, when I am in shock or when things are remarkably good.

I must've been giving you the death stare, like Angelina eyeing Brad before all hell breaks loose. But then I cracked up, all Southern Belle-like, *"Don't worry, I don't bite."*

You looked relieved and asked if I wanted to grab a drink, but I had other plans. *"Nah, I'd rather whoop your butt in some games."*

The look on your face was priceless. *"Huh?"*

"Dave and Busters," I clarified, grinning like a fool.

And whoop your butt, I did, in every game except one. Gotta let you win one time, right? Can't bruise the ego too much on the first date.

As the day went on, you didn't want it to end. But I knew better. *"All good things come to an end, you know?"*

You asked about drinks again, but I shut that down. *"I don't start a drink until after 5."*

That's when you started sweating even more. *"You alright there, champ?"* I asked, wondering if I should be concerned.

You mentioned seeing your grandson Bailey soon but still wanting to meet up later. I was torn between thinking you were a stand-up guy or a total nutjob. But something – maybe the Big Guy himself – told me to give you a shot.

"Round two in a couple of hours?" you asked, hopeful as a kid on Christmas morning.

I played it cool. *"We'll see about that."*

As we braved the February freeze to my car, I couldn't help but bolt ahead, forgetting you were supposed to be my escort. Oops. I slowed my roll, mulling over how cute and nerdy you were, with your good manners and that killer smile.

When we reached my Lexus, you seemed impressed. You said I used to drive a Lexus also.

We said our goodbyes with a quick hug, and you promised to ping me as soon as you were free.

An hour later, true to your word, you texted: *"I'm all yours."*

I dropped my address, and after some GPS drama (seriously, dude?), you finally made it. Little did I know, we'd end up gabbing until the crack of dawn.

We laid it all out there – our past flames, our heartaches, our regrets. Our stories lined up wild, right down to the last name, Tyler. You spilled about Josephine and that restraining order keeping you from Jacob. About June, wife number one, and how she roughed up your boys, Teagan and Carter. How you raised them solo from the get-go.

I shared my baggage – single-momming it with Piper, the Easton Wagner mess, and my stint with Dennis Tyler. We both knew the drill – fighting tooth and nail for our kids, loving them fiercely when the world seemed against us.

You opened up about Jordan, your latest ex, and I could see the hurt in your eyes as you talked about her stepping out and picking her high school flame over you. It was also a coincidence that her name was Jordan Tyler, and she had the same last name as mine, Tyler. My heart went out to you, juggling all those boys on your own after the split.

We bonded over our playlist favs, from Eminem to Snoop and all the old-school beats in between. You even bragged about bumping into Snoop at the Uptown Ballroom in Iowa City.

After 15 hours of nonstop chatter, it felt like we'd known each other forever. We'd put it all on the table – our battles, our victories, our rugrats, our pipe dreams. As the sun peeked over the horizon, I realized something crazy had happened. In you, I'd found my mirror image, someone who'd walked through fire and came out swinging. I might've strolled into that restaurant thinking I'd never fall for a chrome dome, but as I watched you gush about your kids and your wild ride of a life, I realized I was already halfway gone. Falling hard and fast. And you know what? I wouldn't have it any other way.

This is what I'd been dreaming about, day in and day out. If God took me now, I'd go peacefully. When my memory's shot, it'll be pure bliss. Those

90 days and nights were just the warm-up for the next 90 till I'd see you again. And every day after that? Pure magic.

Chapter 5: Father's Day

Happy Father's Day, Sutton Harrington. We're all here together, just as you always pictured - your boys, your grandson, and our blended family. Teagan, Carter, Jacob, Ava, Casey, and Piper are all celebrating you. This is the family portrait you always dreamed of, gathering on holidays like today. There are more to come. We love you, we miss you... Happy heavenly Father's Day, my love. Wish you were here. I made poke bowls for everyone - you'd have demolished three. All your favorites are right there in the bowl.

The boys are out back, playing basketball hard like you always wanted. We made it to Valley Church for Father's Day service, sitting and worshiping as a family, just as you envisioned. Today's been good. Hopeful. We had dinner with my folks and Piper at a Vietnamese restaurant. Now the kids are back at their places... just you and me, baby. Time to relax in the hot tub. Mama needs some chill time.

Earlier, I was teaching Bailey to dance in the hot tub. You'd be so proud. On June 22, we brought your ashes home from Caldwell Parrish Funeral Home in Adel. Having you home with us... it meant everything. That night, June 22, 2024, I saw you so clearly. You came to me and told me to wait 90 days. You and God laid it out for me - finish the mission in 90 days, and I'd get what I've been praying for. All night in my dreams, you reminded me of our first date. Fifteen hours, from 2 p.m. on February 4, 2024, to 5 a.m. on February 5. You recapped everything we talked about and told me, *"You got this, girl."* You said I needed to finish this book by October 22, 2024 - 90 days from when we brought you home. You promised to stay with me until then to help me remember the little details I might forget. God told me my mission was to tell our journey from start to finish.

You wanted me to share our amazing, rare story with the world. From that very first night, when I dozed off around 5 a.m. for barely two hours before you left for work, God spoke to me. You kissed me goodbye and promised a message at lunch. I took the day off initially - I couldn't function on two hours of sleep, though you somehow managed an eight-hour workday. You admitted later you didn't sleep at all, afraid the date would end if you did.

When you got home from work, you told me how you'd stayed up all night, talking to God while I slept. You were astonished and said you'd never seen anything like it - me having a full-blown conversation with God in my sleep. For 90 days after that, we spent nearly every night together. You'd stay up, listening to my sleep-talking, getting by on just four hours of rest. You were determined to know everything about me - my wants, dreams, passions. You swore you'd make it all come true if it was the last thing you did.

Your first text that morning at 9 a.m.: *"Good morning, beautiful. Can't wait to see you after work. All I can do is think about you - it's distracting me from work."* I sent back that *"sorry"* emoji with the woman shrugging. You replied, *"Please don't be sorry. Getting to know you was the best time I've ever had. You're exactly who I've been searching for all my life."* You said the same thing at Hu Hot, and I thought honesty was adorable. My friends thought I was nuts and warned me to be careful - no one says these things after one date. But our date was like 12 dates in one night. That's why it felt like we'd known each other for years.

As I was falling asleep, we both said it felt like we knew each other from a past life. We'd never experienced this kind of connection before - pure, vulnerable, raw. It was almost like the Holy Spirit pushed us together the moment I opened that heavy door at Hu Hot.

I shared my love for God from the get-go. You said you'd never met someone who'd been through so much pain and trauma but still came out smiling, happy, and positive. You asked how I did it, how I put one foot in front of the other every day. I answered, *"I walk with Jesus every day. I talk to Him about every decision I make, especially since 2016 when I found out about Dennis Tyler's affair that blew up our marriage."*

That first night, in my dream, you recounted everything I'd said, matching exactly what I'd heard from God. He told me to write our story, this fairy tale love we'd share for the rest of our lives. God said I'd been waiting all my life for a man like you, that you were a gift, but you needed saving. He warned me never to give up on you; it wouldn't be easy, but it would be worth it. He said we both had to endure all that pain and suffering in our separate lives to unite us. This was my time to love you unconditionally because you'd love me the same way. I've been talking to God since I was eleven, but that night's message was the clearest direction I'd ever received. When I explained all this to you, you said, *"I know, beautiful. I heard it all in your sleep."*

On February 5, my family celebrated my daughter's birthday at Samurai. I was only gone for two hours, but you couldn't wait to see me again. You asked me to pick you up from the Extended Stay Hotel, where you and Teagan were staying. We talked until 3 a.m. again. That night, I dreamed of our future - which was ironic, given my history, easier and happier both our lives might have been if we met in 2005. You wouldn't have met Jordan, and I wouldn't have met Dennis Tyler or other past relationships that promised a future only to deceive us.

Chapter 6: Our Last Conversation

May 4th, 2024. Sutton and I went to the 5 p.m. service at Valley Church. At this point, Sutton was already a member and belonged to this church family.

Something inside of him was awakened and shaken. The Holy Spirit always moves me every time, and I get teary. When I looked over at him holding my hand during the service, I saw that he was experiencing the Holy Spirit himself. Of all the times we've been here, I've never seen him so moved.

I felt a sense of relief for him. I felt God had finally rescued him. That morning, Piper's fire alarm had gone off in her building. I had slept in that Saturday, and she was in a frantic mood, as was Sutton when he took her call. Piper called me, but I was asleep, and Sutton didn't want to wake me up since he knew I needed the rest.

He rushed over to her apartment in 2 minutes, he said - though it takes 6 minutes to get there. Sutton was a superhero for my Piper that day. He burned through every traffic light and stop sign to get to her quickly. Sutton was stressed and overwhelmed by her fear of the alarm going off and his deep love for her and me, and he needed to be the rescue hero for Piper.

He yelled, *"Honey, baby Piper is having an emergency issue. I'm going over to her,"* and ran out the door before I could even open my eyes. I thought I was dreaming. After a couple of minutes, what you had said dawned on me. I jumped off our bed and called my baby girl. She was bawling and scared, thinking her new apartment was going to burn down. Luckily, Sutton was on his way.

After 20 seconds on the phone with her, Sutton arrived and held her. He stayed with her for about half an hour, comforting her and making sure she was calm and safe. This was the first time my daughter had felt afraid for her life since she was 11 years old when she saw a rope hanging in our Minnesota home basement, where her daddy had tried to hang himself.

Sutton, babe, I love you so much for being there for her when neither I nor her daddy could.

He came home relieved but still with a racing heart from all the excitement. He felt like he needed a drink at 11:30 a.m. I was in the shower when he got home, and I could smell the Crown Apple on his breath as soon as he held me when I got out. I knew it had been a terrifying day for him, so I didn't give him any grief about drinking this early. He said he was only having one.

We had lunch and did stuff around the house, like laundry, cleaning up, and unpacking. Under my nose, he drank half a bottle of Crown Apple, not the small bottle but the larger size. He didn't seem out of control or drunk, though. He was always calm and cool about his drinking, among other things. He made a call to the boys to see what they were up to that day and tried to invite them to church with us that evening. I didn't realize he had drunk that much until 4:15 that afternoon, as I was busy around the house while he sat and moped around drinking. I asked for his help unpacking the rest of the stuff, and he said we could finish that tonight, honey. Being the patient, loving Christian woman that I am, I took the high road and said, *"Okay, babe, it's okay. I've got it."* I knew he had been drinking, and I knew how to deal with people who drank too much, as Dennis Tyler had done the same thing that I had struggled with for many years.

Before we left for church, he decided to get sober up for church by smoking a blunt, thinking this would help him get right with himself. As we were getting ready, I suggested, *"Babe, you may want to spray some good stuff so you don't smell like weed or alcohol walking into the church, as my family will also be there."* He seemed very upset with me. I saw the veins on his forehead pop and blow up, and his face instantly turned bright red, and he clenched his fist. No angry words came out of his mouth. He responded, *"Okay, babe, I'll do that."*

He had made a promise to me on day one that he would never mentally, verbally, or physically abuse me in any way. He promised he wouldn't even dare to make me mad or upset because he said I was the best thing he had ever had, and he was too afraid of losing me. His love for me was almost like an addiction of its own. We were addicted to each other in a healthy way, not in a codependent way - at least not for me. I did wonder if that was different for him. He never wanted to leave my side. He wouldn't even let me go to the store by myself, almost as if he was afraid to lose me. He never once yelled at me or raised his voice. Yet, I could see his struggles and his demons coming out. I never once feared for my life or safety with him. I thanked him and told him thank you for putting on some cologne before church.

We went to church and met up with my brother and sister. Pastor Martin was preaching, and he was awakened and moved by his sermon in a way he had never felt before. Sutton squeezed my hand until it left his nail mark. I knew he was in pain, but God had got him.

Before church that morning, I had taken a THC gummy to relax, as I do every day. Yes, I got the okay from my doctor, Dr. Daniel, to take a gummy to deal with my anxiety and depression for relaxation, but only one a day, like a vitamin. For some reason, that gummy hit me like a truck. It lasted all day until the next morning at 8:45 a.m. This gummy lasted almost 20 hours.

On our way out from the church, Sutton mentioned he wanted the lion tattoo *by Donna Elliot on the wall posted at church and said, "Let's get this tattoo now."* I responded, *"We will."* I said,

"Let's go home." On the way out, he was very loud, saying how he finally saw it. He said, *"Babe, I see it now. I see it."* I asked, *"What do you mean?"* He said, *"I've seen the message and our future."* He said, *"I saw God speaking to me for real."* We were in a hurry rushing out of the church, where hundreds of people were getting out, and we felt a bit rushed and overwhelmed. I mentioned, *"Okay, honey, can you tell me all this when we get outside."* He gave me a very disappointed look as if I was dismissing him or thoughtless not to hear him out right at that moment, as he was screaming and telling me this story. I was only trying to keep cool and pay attention to what he was saying because it was loud at the church walking out. I told him I wanted to hear him out but requested that he wait till we were outside. He responded, *"Okay, fine."*

In less than a minute, we were outside. He mentioned that God had told him to always stay true to himself and not fear what other people think or judge. He said, *"You're right; you've been encouraging me to not give two shits about what others think of me."* He also said, *"I truly believe now that God has a plan."*

I responded, *"Yes, he does."*

He continued, *"See, baby, everything has a plan... we are together and soulmates because that was God's plan. What happened with Piper this morning was God's plan, and my speeding to get to her was also God's plan. Everything was in God's hands, as I always said, 'Jesus takes the wheel.'"*

It dawned on me how stressed and overwhelmed he was that he drank so much and smoked a blunt before we left the house for church. At that moment, I remembered asking him to help with laundry. I then asked him what God's plan was in his interpretation. He responded, *"I don't need to worry about anything at all. Everything will fall into place, as you say, babe."* He said, *"If I don't want to go back to work because my boss Sanders wanted me to, because my other boss is pissing me off, then I don't have to because God will always provide and always has our backs."* He said, *"There's no need to stress myself or your beautiful little head anymore."*

I responded, *"Yes, God has a plan, but don't you think we still need to follow the path of goodness and righteousness to lead us to a place where we belong?"* He said, *"No."*

I looked at him with a very puzzled yet scared, alarming look on my face. I felt fear for the first time. He continued, *"We can do what we want, from smoking weed every day, I can take more than one gummy a day to have fun and relax if I want, and drink whenever I feel like it, and tell people to fuck off whenever I think it's valid and needed."* He said, *"As long as we have God in our hearts, God forgives everything."* My face looked even more terrified for his heart, mind, soul, and physical health. I was terrified for him.

I drove home; we got home, and he continued to preach that God had a plan. We got home, and he finished almost the rest of the bottle and found another bottle that I had hidden from him in the laundry room as he had decided to help with chores. I didn't allow him to open that bottle he found. I mentioned to him, *"You've been drinking all morning and night now, and it's Saturday night."* I knew we were going to barbecue with the kids after church for Asian rib night.

I said, *"Hey, babe, hear me out here, okay? Yes, God has a plan for us, and yes, God brought us together when our paths should have crossed in 2005 before he met Jordan. Life could have been so different for us both. But God gives us all these things on earth, good and bad stuff, for us to exist. That doesn't mean we can go buck wild and do what we want. We have choices to make, and those choices are going to determine what kind of life we have on earth and in heaven."*

I explained that *"God will provide and will never abandon us like our earthly parents or people who claim to love us, but we, as God's children, need to follow his word as closely as we can. We are sinners, and yes, we make mistakes, but we learn from those mistakes and don't repeat them again. He wants us to be better. The more we follow his word, the more prosperous our lives will be."* He looked at me with rage and anger and said, *"Let's just have fun."* He hinted that I should take another gummy to get high and have fun.

I said, *"Nah, I'm good."* He was very upset at this point. He yelled, screamed, and said I was righteous, controlling, demanding, and very condescending to him. He said, *"I'm not gonna sit here and listen to this."* He took stuff in a tote that he could grab and carry and said, *"I'm calling Teagan to pick me up."*

I begged him to sober up and sleep it off, and we could talk with a clear mind later. He proceeded to walk out the door. I tried to stop him for a minute, but I saw how angry he was, and his fist clenched up. I blocked the door from him leaving. He said, *"Get out of the way. I will carry you and move you if I have to."*

At this point, I was scared. I never felt so scared for my life since Dennis Tyler. I stepped away and let him leave, and I followed him downstairs for just a second. God spoke to me, saying, *"Let him go in peace to be with Teagan so he can clear his mind."*

Half an hour later, he texted and said he would be in Decorah for a bit to clear his head. He also said, *"Maybe, just maybe, I will stay here..."*

I didn't see his text until 8:45 a.m. the next day. After over 12 hours, I didn't respond to him because I was trying to have my peace and listen to God's word that he needed time to clear his head. I thought he was safe with Teagan until I read the message. We messaged all day Sunday. We worked it all out.

That was one of my last words. I let him have his space and help with Carter around 4 p.m. I messaged him, asking, *"I'm guessing you're still with Carter. What do you want me to do with these ribs?"* He responded, *"Give Teagan for dinner."*

I went about my business and fell asleep, only to be awoken by Carter's phone call at 1:30 am, but I didn't get to answer quickly enough. I was groggy and sleepy, so I went back to bed. I didn't realize Carter had called until Teagan woke me at 3 am and said, *"Dad is gone, Joslyn!"* I was puzzled and said, *"What are you talking about? He's in Decorah with Carter."* Teagan then said, *"He shot himself, Joslyn!"*

I took half of the gummy by lunchtime and the other half when he sent me the song at 3:45 pm the night before to calm my nerves because I didn't want to act anxious around my parents during lunch for my mom's birthday. When Teagan woke me up, I was still a little delusional; it was 3 am. I passed out to sleep again.

I woke up around 7 am, realized what a night it had been, and remembered everything. I called Teagan and told him he was lying and that there was no way in hell for Sutton to do that. I know Sutton, and he would never leave us like that. I did not believe it and did not want to believe it. I told Teagan that the only way I would believe it was if I saw his dead body. Teagan said his head was blown off, Joslyn. I said, *"I don't care. I need to see him."*

I drove to Teagan and repeated the same crap I had said earlier. I called my Piper and told her. I drove to Decorah to Carter's, rang the bell, and no one answered. The driveway didn't seem to be disturbed much, or maybe I just refused to see it. There was no blood on the driveway, the siding, or the green car parked. I sat on the ground, begging to find him. I saw a pool of blood and some brain fragments on the grass. I started screaming, begging God, *"Please don't let this happen to him. Please, he can't be dead."*

Casey's brother came out. I said, *"He didn't die here. This didn't happen. Please tell me this didn't happen."* He said, *"I'm sorry, it happened this morning at about 1:30 am."*

Chapter 7: To Be A Man

To be a man was your favorite song, babe. Remember, we'd stay up for hours, both singing it off the top of our lungs? The first time I heard it was when you showed me what you'd sent your dad, Gerald, months before, after you got shot in August 2023.

I remember how heartbroken you were when you didn't hear back from him about the song. You felt defeated when your father wasn't able to understand the real you. I thought it was the most beautiful thing anyone had ever shared with me.

You were raw, broken, and vulnerable with me and this song, plus your stories of your entire life. I knew God had sent you just for me; that moment, I listened to this song while you sang it at the top of your lungs. We forever bonded over the same anxiety, fear, and depression of not feeling enough.

You said to me, *"I don't want this bad world to know you; I want to keep you safe in your bubble for as long as I can or die trying. I don't want anything to hurt you, not my past, present, or future; you've been through more trauma and pain than anyone I know, yet you're strong, fearless, ballsy, smart as a whip, determined to succeed, and not to mention beautiful, gorgeous inside and out."* At that moment, I felt truly loved for the first time.

"Your positivity and drive in life, especially the certainty you feel about your Jesus, is remarkable to me. Your love for Jesus and love for me is something I will cherish all my life. You're always full of smiles and have shown me more compassion, kindness, and, most of all, grace, the way Jesus can," you went on.

We shared the same love language at every level. We shared almost every minute of our day with each other, besides work and Bailey time. We found each other at the right time when we needed it most. I showed you God's love, and you showed me your love for me. I knew this was God's plan for us.

The love we shared was like no other. I saw the real you on the first day we met. Finding a partner who can be honest and transparent about his feelings and fears with me is rare. You poured your heart out to me from the moment we locked eyes.

I was madly in love with you that night you sang this song. This song gave me more appreciation for my own dad and how he did his best to provide for his family. We must have sung it together almost every night. I saw your soul, and you saw mine. From that moment on, we were truly, madly in love.

You said, *"It's a feeling you've never felt before,"* and I said, *"Ditto, honey,"* then you proceeded to put boyz II men on bended knees as we danced together. Our lives were perfect. We were imperfectly in love together, with all our flaws, anxiety, and fear of not being enough. You said we are enough together, and who cares what the world thinks?

You were overly protective of your past with the shooting in August 2023, hiding me from the entire social media so the people who shot you would not find me. You were too concerned that your past would hurt me. Even though you were so protective, you showed me your life in Decorah and Adel. I met your acquaintances and friends from your past and really understood the kind of man you were. You said, *"I'm proud to show you off to everyone."* I knew then that I was never a secret; I was your present and future.

The way you spoke of all your boys – Teagan Harrington, Carter Harrington, Jacob Clark, Bailey, and Caleb - was pure love, and that made me see the whole you that no one had ever seen before. You're one proud and loving father to all your Harrington boys.

I wished my Piper had a father who loves her fiercely like you love your boys. Her biological dad is not in her life, and he never wanted to be. It was always Piper and me against the world, even after Dennis came into our lives. I felt safe the moment you came into my life. You loved her and were overly protective of her like she always had you as a dad. You asked, and I answered with a yes: *"Will you let me be a dad to your baby girl?"* You said, *"I never had a daughter; I only produce boys. Obviously, I would be honored to love your Piper while her dad is protecting her from up there. I will protect her down here."*

That's when I knew we were home. I admire your dedication and love for your boys so much that I knew I had found my person. We connected like no one has ever connected before. You woke up something inside of me that needed to be awakened.

I brought you home to meet my parents. You saw my dad's heart and saw what a good father he is, as he loved me so much he felt the need to protect me from you. My parents didn't get the chance to really know the real you, and that's too bad; I guess it was their loss. You saw my mom's pain and disapproval of you that triggered some bad memories of your past relationship of not being accepted by the family of the person you thought you once loved.

You saw the anguish and the hurt I felt because my parents didn't approve of my choice to be with you, and I felt so heartbroken for you. You saw the control they had on my life and the pain I suffered all my life. You saw the pain I felt because, yet again, my parents were dissatisfied with my actions, like I was a criminal. You made me see my value and my own heart. You showed me how to be proud of myself, as you were proud to call me your future wife.

You gave me the strength to be honest with my mom for the first time. You even typed the words out for me to message her and had it translated to Filipino; I don't write Filipino well, and it's always a struggle to have my parents truly understand the real me. You know, the only love I seek besides God's love is of my mother and father. I always felt like I'm just not good enough in their eyes. You saw my struggle with my anxiety, PTSD, and depression, which flared up after my dad walked into our apartment; you stood by my side always. To be fair, my forgetful brain left the key on the door, which allowed him permission to come in without calling. Oopsey daisy, my bad....

You made sure I took my medication on time, ate three meals a day, and called me every hour to make sure I hadn't gone completely nuts off my rocker. Dr. Daniel told me to take two weeks off work to reflect and regulate myself in April. You are the most attentive, loving husband I could have asked for.

No one gets me like you do. You struggled with the same anxiety and fear yourself. I thought to myself and spoke to God, *"Only if my family knew the kind of heart you had that beats so loud, like the sound of drums in my ear."* I knew at that moment that you were real. You don't fake love.

You're such a strong man; you put your own fears aside of my parents' disapproval and comforted me. You said, *"If I were your dad, I would be fiercely protective of you too because you're an amazing daughter, mother, best friend, sister, and wife that he could ever ask for."* You said, *"Be glad that they worry about you and never once abandoned you; I will be the same kind of father to Piper as your dad is to you."* That's when we thought we couldn't love each other more than that moment.

Every day was a new chapter in our lives, and I promised myself on the first night that we had the kind of fairy tale love that we had dreamed about our entire lives and were seeking but looking in the wrong places. Suppose our paths had crossed when I went to Adel in 2005 with Jill. How different our lives would be and how happy our family would be. But it wasn't God's plan. What we had was God's plan. The plan is to love each other unconditionally so that our love will last forever, even after death, when we will be together again.

The first night, I dreamed of our entire life as you lay next to me, listening to me all night. That's why you were too tired to go to work the next morning. You stayed up listening and talking in my dream about us, the promise I made that our love story was one of a kind. God spoke to me that night and said, *"This is your story, and the world should know."* We were not Romeo and Juliet or West Side Story... We were Sutton and Joslyn, like Rocky to his Adrienne!

I know God brought you to me in the last few months of your life because we both needed healing together. You are my rock, and I am your wave in the ocean. Together, we are unstoppable. My world and my family grew from just Piper and me against the world to you fighting the world to protect us all. I never felt so safe and loved by anyone until you.

There were many nights we stayed up and talked all night about everything. We had to pinch ourselves to make sure that it wasn't a dream. You had the rubber band bracelet saying *"not satisfied yet"* on you, always snapping it to make sure we were not dreaming. Everything felt like a dream. We laughed, cried, and danced to all the music like no one was around. Everything always felt right and natural to us. We used to say how addicted we were to each other, and it felt right because we were honest to ourselves and each other about what was in our hearts, with no fear of judgment or abandonment.

It always felt like we knew each other from a past life. When we took you home from Caldwell Parrish Funeral Home, I felt the first night we were together all over again; it reminded me of our life together, and I went down the first-date memory lane in my subconscious mind for the 15 hours we spent together. That's when you shouted out, *"Let's get married here and now."* You made that palm leaf we got from the church into a ring. We got married in our kitchen while we pigged out on everything we had in the kitchen except the Sunday spoon.

I wish we had just done it and maybe moved to Florida, as we talked about in April. Plans were already in the works, movers were hired, and we even started packing. We planned to marry right when we got to Tampa. I'm sorry we didn't move, as you wanted so badly to be close to your dad, Gerald. I'm sorry, but I got in my head and convinced you that we should wait for all the seasons. I was always in my head, weighing every decision's pros and cons. That's why we were perfect together; I overthink things before I make a decision, and you were always the *"fly by the seat of your pants"* kind of guy. We balanced each other out like yin and yang. God spoke to me that night, saying, *"You hang on to him and put your running shoes away. You can stop running; instead, take walks on the ocean with him for the rest of your life."* I envisioned our entire life in one dream. I dreamt of our life that night, and of course, I always talked in my sleep. The next morning, you said, *"Babe, you talked about everything in your sleep. I can see our future."*

That's when we knew that God had brought us together to heal and love each other like we were one heart and one soul. This is our story. I'm gonna call it the *"Gucci Gang Story."* I promise there is a reason for my madness to call it that, but a good one.

The *"Gucci Gang"* moniker originated from our cherished weekly Wednesday wing nights at Wellman's rooftop bar. One of the Asian sauces, pronounced *"Gucci gang"* but spelled differently (possibly *"goudgzang"*), became your favorite. You always said it reminded you of me - *"sweet, spicy, tangy, with just the right amount of kick, all in one bite."* Soon, *"Gucci"* became your go-to word for anything good. We even considered naming our story *"The Gucci Gang Story."*

It helped that Gucci was our shared favorite brand for sunglasses and purses. After you left this world, I adopted a kitten and named her Gucci in your memory. Her companion, fittingly, is named Prada. I'm only a Louis Vuitton away from completing my designer kitten trio - a whimsical tribute to our favorite brands. This book's title, *"The Gucci Gang Story,"* encapsulates it all - the sauce that reminded you of your true love, our shared passions, and the bittersweet memories we created together.

Chapter 8: Our Special Place

It had been a hectic week since you had returned from the funeral home. That Friday night, when we moved into our new apartment, we were determined to finish everything and celebrate afterward. As we pulled up to our new place at Cliff Space, the sight of the hot tub, surrounded by yellow tape and a tarp, was too much for you to resist.

"Let's just go for it," you said, that familiar mischievous grin spreading across your face. Without hesitation, you asked, *"Did you ask for God's permission?"* And to our surprise, He seemed cool with it. Asked and answered.

As we stepped into the hot, bubbling water, the weight of the day's chaos melted away. We sat there, gazing up at the stars, making plans to do this every night. It felt like the start of a new chapter in our lives, a chance to truly connect and enjoy the simple pleasures.

The moment was electric as if the universe had aligned just for us. We talked about our dreams, our fears, and everything in between. It was as if we had known each other for decades, sharing a bond that transcended time and space. You asked me to be patient with you and not give up on you, and I promised I would always be by your side.

That night, we truly became one, our souls intertwined in a way that defied explanation. The 26-foot U-Haul parked nearby didn't even faze us – we were lost in our own little world, oblivious to the curious glances from the patios nearby. At that moment, nothing else mattered except the two of us basking in the glow of our newfound intimacy. As I look back on that night, I can't help but smile. I remember the way we sat in that same spot, the one you had claimed as your own, gazing up at the stars until closing time. We were so lost in our own little world that we didn't even notice the people around us.

Life got busy after that night, and our hot tub adventures became fewer and farther between. But I never forgot that first night, how we connected so deeply, how we felt like we had known each other for a lifetime. It was a moment that would forever be etched in my heart, a reminder of the strength and resilience of our love.

Even now, as I sit here in this same spot, I can't help but feel a sense of nostalgia. I almost want to put up a sign, *"Do not sit here. The Holy Spirit of Sutton claims this spot. Beware of trespassers."* But then I remember the promise we made that night to respect the rules and not cause any harm. You always kept that promise, even after you were gone.

It's been a tumultuous journey since then, filled with both joy and sorrow. The demons that took over my head in the weeks after your passing were relentless, and I struggled to find my faith. I prayed every day, afternoon and night, for you to come home, but it felt like God wasn't listening.

Then, thinking about your birthday on May 20th, something shifted. At a Willy Nelson concert, I felt God's presence like never before. It was as if you were there, beside me, telling me that everything was going to be okay, that I had this, that you believed in me. God spoke to me then, reminding me of the mission He entrusted me – to love you unconditionally and help heal our boys. I was both relieved and terrified, unsure of my ability to carry out such a monumental task. But then I remembered the night we moved in, the way we connected, the way you asked me to be patient and not give up on you.

That night, the night we first tried the hot tub, was the night we really connected on the next chapter of our lives. It was as if we had known each other for decades, you and I, sharing a bond that was deeper than anything we had ever experienced. You were a man of mystery, and I was eager to learn more about you and understand your soul's depths.

As I sit here now, I can't help but remember the moments we shared, the laughter, the tears, the mistakes we made. After your passing, I learned so much about you, things that the boys and others who knew you shared with me. But God reminded me that the only memories that truly matter are the ones I had with you, the ones I hold close to my heart.

It's been a difficult journey, navigating the grief and the anger that consumed me in the days and weeks after you were gone. I felt like I had lost my faith, like I couldn't hear God's voice the way I normally could. I remember those long, sleepless nights, especially kneeling on the floor of Summer's home that one night, crying out to God, begging Him to bring you back to me. But then, just as I was about to give up, God spoke to me, reminding me of the mission He had entrusted to me. He told me, ‘ You needed saving and that it was my job to love you unconditionally, to accept you for all of your flaws because you had the heart of Jesus.’It was as if He had been preparing me for this moment all along, guiding me through the difficult relationships and the choices I had made in the past.

As I write this, I can’t help but think about the lessons we’ve learned, the mistakes we’ve made, and the growth we’ve experienced. We may not have been perfect, but our love was. And ultimately, that’s what matters most. I may have lost you on this earth, but I’ll never lose the memories we created, the bond we shared, and the legacy we left behind.

This morning, Carter, Casey, and I went to the 11 am service at our church. The sermon was all about Peter, one of the twelve disciples of Jesus, and his struggle to trust in the Lord. It reminded me so much of our journey, the way we sometimes doubted and sometimes strayed but always found our way back to the path of faith.

Just like Peter, we had our moments of doubt and fear, but God always reached out his hand, offering us the chance to take hold and be saved. That's what He's doing for me now, reminding me that I'm not alone in this mission, that you are guiding me, and that together, we can heal our family and honor the legacy you left behind.

So, here I am, sitting in our special spot, looking up at the stars, and knowing that you are with me. I can almost hear your voice telling me that You got this, that you believe in me. And I'm determined to carry out this mission, one day at a time, with the strength and resilience that you always embodied. As I remember that first hot tub night, I can't help but smile at the memories we created. The way we broke the rules, connected on a level that defied explanation, and made plans to do it every night – it all feels like a lifetime ago. But the love, bond, and memories will live on forever as our love will last for eternity and beyond.

I may have lost you, but I'll never lose the piece of you that lives on in our boys, in our family, and in my heart. This is our mission and purpose, and I'm honored to carry it out, honor your legacy, and continue the journey we started that fateful night in the hot tub. Because in the end, that's what truly really matters most – the love we shared, the memories we created, and the lives we touched.

Chapter 9: Our Special Place (Part 2)

The warm, bubbling water of the hot tub enveloped us, and as we sat there gazing up at the stars, I couldn't help but feel a profound sense of gratitude. Just two years ago, I had been at my lowest point, battling illness with my brain cancer and feeling completely alone. But now, here I was, with you by my side, embarking on a new chapter of our lives.

As we talked about our dreams and fears, I couldn't help but reflect on the journey that had brought us to this moment. I remembered the promise I had made to God, the one where I vowed to make amends with everyone I had wronged if He saved my life. And when He did, it was as if a weight had been lifted off my shoulders.

But then, just like you, I was abandoned by someone I thought loved me during the most fragile time of my life. It was a betrayal that cut deep, leaving me feeling lost and uncertain. But through it all, I held onto my faith, knowing that God would never abandon me, just as He had never abandoned you.

Your story and your struggles resonated with me on a level I couldn't fully explain. I saw the pain and the trauma you had endured, the way people had turned their backs on you, just as they had done to me. But through it all, you never lost your faith, your unwavering belief in the power of God's love. As we sat in the hot tub, I couldn't help but feel a deep connection to you. We were both works in progress, imperfect humans trying to navigate the complexities of life. But at that moment, it didn't matter. All that mattered was the love and the bond we shared, a bond that transcended time and space.

The show called The Chosen taught me the story of Simon Peter and how he struggled with the loss of his unborn child while he was away doing Jesus' work to follow him. I could see the parallels in your own life, the way you had grappled with the pain, and the questions of why God would allow such suffering to happen to those who followed Him.

But then, I am reminded of the power of forgiveness, of the way Jesus died on the cross to absolve us of our sins. I was reminded that we are all imperfect, flawed beings and that the devil likes to confuse us, to make us doubt our faith. But through it all, God remains steadfast, offering us the chance to repent and start anew.

I listened intently, my heart swelling with emotion as you shared your journey, your struggles, and your ultimate surrender to God's plan. You told me that you had learned and repented of your sins and that God had seen the changes you had made in your life, even when those who claimed to love you couldn't.

You mentioned how misguided you were for many years, but after losing your grandma Barbara, you had to learn to be on your own and finally understood her saying to let go of the anger and let God protect us all. Surrender all your worries to Jesus. I was so proud of your realization and how I met you at the exact time. You were transformed into the new and improved Sutton when we met.

And then, as if a veil had been lifted, I finally understood the true depth of your sacrifice. You weren't just a man I had fallen in love with, but a vessel for God's plan, a sacrificial lamb who was willing to give up everything to bring healing and salvation to those you loved.

At that moment, I was filled with a sense of awe and reverence. You had been through so much and endured so much pain and betrayal, yet you still had the strength and courage to surrender yourself to God's will. It was a testament to the power of your faith and the unwavering love you had for me and your family.

As we sat there, the warm water soothing our souls, I knew that this moment, this first hot tub night at our special place, would be forever etched in my memory. It was a night of profound realization, deep connection, and love that transcended this world's boundaries.

I may not have all the answers, and the question of why God allows such suffering to exist may continue to plague me. But in that moment, I knew that I had been blessed with a love that was truly extraordinary, a love that had the power to heal and transform.

And as I look back on that night, I'm reminded of the words you had spoken to me about never abandoning the people you love. You were right;

God never abandons His children, and I vow never to abandon you or your legacy. Together, we will continue to honor your sacrifice, share your story, and inspire others to find the same depths of faith and love that you possess.

This is our mission, our purpose, and I'm honored to carry it out, to be the vessel through which your voice can be heard, your light can shine, and your love can continue to transform the lives of those around us. Because in the end, that's the true meaning of a one-of-a-kind story – the love we shared, the memories we created, and the lives we touched.

As I reflect on that night in the hot tub, I'm reminded of the journey we've been on, the ups and downs, the triumphs and the tragedies. But through it all, our love remained steadfast, a beacon of hope in the darkness.

I remember the way you would hold me and whisper in my ear, telling me that everything was going to be okay. You had a way of calming my fears, of reassuring me that even in the midst of the storm, God was still in control.

And now, as I sit here in this same spot, I can almost feel your presence beside me. It's as if you're telling me that you're still here, that you're still guiding me, still inspiring me to continue on this journey.

The boys, they've been through so much. I see the pain and the confusion in their eyes, the questions that linger unanswered. But I know that you're watching over them, that you're working through me to help them heal, to help them find their way. It's been a long and difficult road, but I'm determined to honor your legacy, share your story, and inspire others to find the same depths of faith and love that you possess. In the end, that's what truly matters – the impact we leave behind, the lives we touch, and the love we share.

As I sit here gazing up at the stars, I can't help but feel a sense of peace and purpose. I know that God has a plan for me, for us, and that even in the midst of the darkness, there is always a glimmer of light.

So I'll keep pushing forward, one day at a time, trusting in the Lord and holding onto the memories we created, the bond we shared. Because, in the end, that's all we really have – the love we give, the lives we touch, and the legacy we leave behind.

Chapter 10: Finding Freedom in Our Faith

Teagan, Ava, and Bailey came to the 11 am service at Valley Church this morning. Bailey got to meet new friends at the Sunday daycare. When I asked him who the names of the people he met were, all he could say was, *"I was friends with the black boy."* A child's mind amazes me, and I burst out laughing so loudly. Then he said, *"Yeah, Grandma Josey,"* with such conviction like he was a grown man in a child's body. This melted my heart. I had always dreamed of having a Caucasian blonde boy, but I knew that would never happen with my Asian descent.

Carter and Casey weren't feeling their best this morning, so they took the weekend off from church. They have been coming with me every Sunday or Saturday for nearly six weeks, and I am so proud of them. They even came to the revival services on Thursdays to learn more about healing.

Today's sermon was about Paul, who was not one of the Twelve Disciples. He was an Apostle who did not know Jesus during his lifetime.

According to the book of Acts, he was a Pharisee who persecuted the early disciples of Jesus. This was especially poignant for Teagan to hear.

What I took away from the sermon was that we need to see others the way Jesus sees us instead of through our own limited perspective. Our perspective can be misleading, colored by our pride, shame, and fear. Pastor Jerome Johnston at Valley Church preached about how we often feel free and stuck at the same time. Living in this world, we have mixed feelings and frequently make poor choices. We never truly feel completely free, as there is always something holding us back. After all, we are all sinners. This is why Jesus died on the cross for our sins, pains, and sufferings - to give us the eternal life we crave for those who turn to him.

The pastor talked about his experience going to the 4TH July fireworks at Commons Park and how they had planned in advance how to park and leave efficiently, avoiding the crowds. He used this as an analogy for how we may feel free because of our earthly freedoms, but life still throws us curve balls that make us feel stuck, burdened, worried, and grieved. It’s important that we surround ourselves with good people who will guide us on the path that brings us closer to God. The moral is that we all need positive influences in our lives because life is not going to be perfect - there will always be troubles and pain. As long as we have a support system of godly people, they can show us the right path to salvation.

Most of the time, we need others in our lives to point us toward the greener pastures. God puts people in our lives for a reason, just like he brought you and me together for the last three months of your precious life. I believe wholeheartedly that God placed you in my life to help guide you to have complete freedom in your heart and to accept him fully. That's why we embarked on our 90-day journey, which was our most amazing experience. In return, you helped me love myself completely, without the fear and judgment that had been holding me back all my life, which stemmed from my family. You brought Piper and me closer in our relationship; we had both been broken for several years after the divorce and her dad's passing. I know that you are undoubtedly finally happy, free, and at peace with Jesus. We realized on day one that we were kindred spirits, kept apart all these years only to find each other during the most opportune time when we needed each other the most. Love is not measured by the amount of time we have known each other - our souls have been searching for one another since 2005.

Often, we are not honest with ourselves or the people who love us about how we are truly doing. When our loved ones ask how we are, we usually say, *"Fine."* But *"fine"* often doesn't mean we are actually fine - it means we don't want to talk about or share what is really bothering us as we bottle things up.

This leads to anger and resentment towards the people we love. This is a common reason why many relationships fail - we are not honest about our true feelings. People say *"fine"* to avoid dealing with the real issues of the heart and mind; we tend to avoid them because we don't want to take responsibility for our wrongdoings and face our mistakes.

A large part of your life was spent saying you were *"fine"* because you were too afraid for others to see your real pain. I don't blame you one bit - sometimes, the people who claim to love us or care about us give off the vibe that they don't want to be *"troubled"* by our problems, as they have their own. At times, it is only our own perception of what we think they are feeling. We project our negative feelings about ourselves onto others and assume they, too, feel ashamed of us. Seeing others the way Jesus sees us is what we all should strive for so our perceptions are not always so negative. The truth is if the people who claim to love and care about you will always reach out - they will never give up or abandon you.

My family never really abandoned me like your experience with yours. Many people in your life failed and abandoned you, starting with your father. You and I relate to this, as my father failed me too. I have wanted to have a close relationship with my dad ever since I can remember. I wanted to hear him tell me he loves me and is proud of me, to sit on his lap as a child, and to laugh together. I don't blame my dad anymore, as I was the cause of what I thought was him not loving me since I turned on him when I was three years old. That was because I was taught to hate him by my own mother, who was hurting in her own pain from her struggles with her own father.

You had people abandon you from as early as when you were a baby when you and your mom would stay home with no food to eat because your earthly father would play in a band and stay out all night eating steaks and partying with his friends as a priority. No child should ever feel that kind of pain, and no wife should ever feel so abandoned by their husband. Of all my dad's flaws, he never abandoned my mom or any of us. He was taught tough love, and the only way he knew how to show it was through discipline, which was the way his father had taught him. It took me a very long time to truly understand my own father.

We all make mistakes, but the ultimate suffering your mother endured was being left by your father to raise you on her own. She did the best she could, and you told me many times how much you loved her, even when it was hard to hear at times. You used to call me *"Diane"* when I initially thought it was an insult until I understood your deep love for her. You admitted to me how much I remind you of her - her fearlessness and bravery are what drew you to me. The saying that every man finds his true love in the image of his first love, his mother, holds so much truth that we all refuse to see until we have accepted and forgiven our mothers for their mistakes. She wasn't perfect and may have made mistakes, but she never gave up on you, and you admitted that to me a few days after we moved into our new place.

As a child, we are not mature enough to see the big picture of what our parents did for us. Even as grown-ups, we still do not have the full maturity we claim to possess. Maturity is something we can never outgrow - we grow and learn until the day we die. We tend to only look at the pain our parents caused us. As a mother, I learn from Piper more and more each day - she has taught me to be cooler and how to be a better parent. As a child, I was always told that parents never make mistakes, and we have to be obedient toward our father and mother, always listening to their teachings. But what do you do when your parents are also misguided? Most of the time, the parent who shows you the most tough love is the one who only wants what's best for you, to allow you to be your own person. Yes, they make mistakes, but don't we all? That does not define you as a person. No matter how much tough love your parents gave you, they always had the best intentions unless they truly abandoned you and stepped away from their responsibilities. Life can deal you the worst cards, but with God and faith, we make the best of what we have and play the hand we were dealt.

God puts people in our paths to teach us lessons, but it may not seem like a lesson until tragedy happens. We need to seek God even when things are good, not only when we are in crisis. When we met, you struggled with that in your heart. I believe it's not because you weren't ready or didn't love God enough. I believe it's the devil taking over your mind and tricking you into believing certain things that may or may not be true. Sometimes, our perceptions of others get messy because we don't choose to see them the way Jesus sees us. We make judgments of others that are not true or real - we only see the worst in people instead of trying to see the best the way God sees us.

The readily available alcohol and drugs in this world did not help your situation. This is why this world we live in is so toxic, but we have a choice to walk with Jesus or the devil. As humans, we think of the worst because we live in a corrupt world where money, fame, and power are treated as the social status that defines success and happiness. Social media markets alcohol, fame, physical beauty, sex appeal, and financial wealth as the true definition of happiness. I remember you said you drank more often than smoking weed occasionally to relax your mind, as that's what society accepts. Society looks down on using marijuana as medicine to heal what's broken.

People like you and me, who have been through so much pain and suffering and deal with PTSD, anxiety, and depression every day, sometimes need certain natural medicines instead of the drugs doctors prescribe. I'm not arguing that doctors over-medicate us, but in some cases, that has happened. Our bodies rely too much on artificial medicine that only helps pharmaceutical companies get wealthy. There are doctors out there who don't really care about their patients, only wanting to fix them with pills. I'm not one to judge, as I've been on prescribed pills since I was 20 years old - over half my life, I've relied on them to save my sanity and help me sleep. With medication, it still takes me 2-3 hours to fall asleep every night. Everything changed when you came into my life. I fell asleep quickly and peacefully every night during the 90 days I was with you.

Yes, I took gummies every day to help with my anxiety when we were together, and that helped me sleep without my prescribed pills. I felt hopeful that I could eventually get off the pills I'd been taking for over 26 years. I tried to smoke marijuana a couple of times with you, but it always made me sick and nauseous, so I preferred the gummies. We even made gummies at home that stunk up the apartment for over a week - your gummies were the best, as you made them for me because you knew they helped me sleep and relax. Relaxing and calming my mind was so hard when I always felt like the world was judging me, but I only cared about how my parents and brothers judged me.

I'm not saying that smoking marijuana recreationally is the best choice, but this corrupted world puts mental illness at the top of the list of why people commit suicide. If I had known how much marijuana could have helped me 20 years ago, I wouldn't have attempted suicide three times and, in turn, hurt the people who love me, starting with Piper. When I found out about Dennis's affair, I was filled with anger, disappointment, and self-doubt about who I was as a person, wife, and mother. I felt like I was never good enough, that he had to seek attention from others on social media and Craigslist to get laid. I was terrified for my health and the diseases I may have contracted as a result.

The gaslighting and lack of responsibility taken by Dennis put me in a desperate situation where I thought taking my own life was the best option. Narcissistic behavior in people doesn't just come overnight - people don't wake up and decide to become narcissistic. Their life experiences and lack of support from family and friends shape them. Just because one person displays bad behavior doesn't mean they were born that way. God created us all beautifully in our uniqueness. Life circumstances make us who we are today. Fully understanding and comprehending what's in our minds to make the right decisions doesn't come immediately - our life experiences shape how we think. I'm not saying we should condone narcissistic behavior in everyone. We must see people for who they are and guard our hearts wisely on who we love. The person you find may not have those behaviors in the beginning, but once you notice them, it's time to ask yourself: is this what God wants for me? Sometimes, people show narcissistic tendencies, but it doesn't make them narcissists - it just shows they need help and are struggling. This is when it's always important to have a relationship with God to bounce ideas off and get good advice from the Almighty.

Often, humans fail other humans, and we blame it on God or religion. But it's not about religion but our faith and beliefs in our Lord. It's not God who failed us - human beings fail each other. Ever since I experienced my first pain and trauma, I was devastated and had no one to turn to but God. The inspiration I had to accept Jesus in my heart fully was shattered by my earthly father when I was eleven. For over 30 years, I blamed him for all my pain and suffering, harboring hate towards my father for the majority of my life. Even though I accepted Jesus in my heart at eleven, I was still a child, and my brain and emotions were not fully developed. It was my parent's job to nurture my faith instead of taking it away; where I felt lost as a child and attempted suicide at 15 by taking two bottles of Tylenol PM and laying naked in the bathroom, hoping to die. I wanted God to take me as I came into this world - naked, with nothing but my soul. After taking those pills, I was incoherent and called my best friend Avery, who kept me on the phone and saved me from falling asleep, where my brain could have shut off, and I wouldn't have woken up. I guess God wasn't done with me yet, even though I had given up on myself. This was my first suicide attempt. God saved me, but I didn't know the full details of who I called that night until recently after you died, when Avery reminded me of that phone call that saved my life. It was God speaking through her to save me from myself.

Fast forward to when I was 23 to 26 years old - I did a lot of drugs during that period of my life. I went out and drank myself stupid nearly every day after working double shifts, first at Hooters, then Daytona's, and finally ended up working at the bars. Every weekend for almost two years, I would take ecstasy from Friday to Sunday, trying to recoup my body and mind on Sunday. From 1 pill to 2 to 3 a night, I was the thinnest I've ever been during that time, barely 82 lbs., as the drugs curbed my appetite. I wouldn't eat from Friday to Monday.

At that time, I also struggled with how I saw myself - all my life, being told I was not good enough and would never amount to anything, that I was ugly, really shattered my self-esteem. Growing up, my mother always compared me to her youngest sister and how thin and slender she was compared to me. She always made me feel like I wasn't worthy of her love in comparison to her sister, who was most elegant, perfect, and flawless in her eyes; I turned out to be nothing but a disappointment to her. I looked in the mirror; I only saw a fat, ugly, overweight, and uneducated woman who didn't deserve to be loved. Taking those ecstasy pills was my way to diet and stay thin in order to bring my confidence back. It helped me escape all the bad qualities I believed I possessed because that's how she always sees me.

I was also a cocaine addict when I was 18 to 20 years old, during my first marriage to Alkaline. I married him for the wrong reasons - only for the drugs and the exciting party life. Luckily, I was able to kick that addiction without any help from rehab or attempting suicide. I was career-driven, and I always had Jesus in my heart, which is what saved me during those times. I saw Alkaline nearly overdose in front of me, and that really woke me up. Even though I went through those struggles, I was still able to focus and function in my career. I had a career at 18 years old and was able to work and still make a comfortable living.

My anxiety and fear of not being able to survive and be the best at what I was taught to be got the better of me. My parents got in my head; luckily, they did because that saved me. They distanced themselves from me for almost two years during my brief six months of marriage to Alkaline, as I was making bad choices. Even my own brother didn't acknowledge my existence when he saw me at a local fair - that's when I realized I was ashamed of who I was.

My anxiety and fear of never being good enough for my parents really messed with my head. I was taught to always be perfect and never make mistakes, which took control of my life. I felt so out of control that I needed ecstasy to feel happy and cope, even after my hard lesson with cocaine at 18. The abuse - verbal, mental, emotional, and eventually physical - really tore me down. I chose to leave Alkaline and moved to Iowa City to work for Franklin restaurant management. I had a successful career that I was proud of and hung on for dear life. I know what struggle feels like ever since I was three years old - not to mention the constant bullying I experienced as an Asian-American moving to this country, always feeling like I never belonged anywhere, being afraid to sleep at night due to nightmares of my family fighting and arguing, being told I was useless and would never amount to anything.

Chapter 11: A Love Born from Pain

Growing up, I never felt truly accepted by my own parents. No matter how hard I try to be the perfect, obedient Asian daughter, I always feel short of their love. They taught me to keep my feelings inside and never speak to anyone about my true emotions. They were ashamed of me, and maintaining the image of a perfect family was paramount. I couldn't even share my feelings with my grandparents, aunts, or uncles because my parents feared judgment. Other people's opinions mattered most.

I lived in constant fear, especially after we moved to Iowa. If I didn't sweep the floor perfectly, leaving no dust behind, I'd get beaten with the same broom - a lesson I'd never forget. To this day, I'm obsessive about cleaning, still getting down on my hands and knees to feel if the floor is smooth. My mom would be disappointed if I didn't make potstickers perfectly, with no holes or punctures. She'd call me useless if I didn't roll egg rolls flawlessly. No matter how hard I tried, it was never good enough in their eyes.

This upbringing made me obsessed with perfection. I expected it from myself for a long time, never allowing any errors. I blamed myself more harshly than others ever could. In a way, this gave me an unparalleled work ethic. Always fearing failure and disappointing those around me, I worked myself to the bone for most of my life. Giving up was never an option. I constantly strived to be the best in everything I did. My success didn't come from thin air - it came from hard work, discipline, and, most importantly, my love for God, which kept me sane. When my parents bought their first restaurant, I was 14. Before that, they had run a catering business from home for years. Since I was 10 or 11, it was my specific duty to wash all the pots and pans and clean the entire kitchen - stove, oven, counters, and floors. On top of that, I cared for my younger brother, from picking him up from school to feeding him and giving him baths. I had to be an adult before I even became a teenager.

If I showed any unhappiness on my face, I'd be yelled at and told I was ungrateful for the roof over my head and the food on the table. My dad would threaten that if he had known I'd be such a disappointment, he would have choked me to death and left me in a dumpster when I was born. I was nothing but a piece of shit in his eyes. My mother never protected me from him, even though since I was three years old, my whole childhood had been about protecting her from him.

I worked all my life from the age of eleven, doing homework while peeling onions and garlic. My mother taught me to be a housewife at eleven. I knew how to cook at a young age and perfected the art of cleaning. Anything less than spotless was unacceptable. It's funny how they didn't have the same expectations for my older or younger brothers. My brothers' words were gospel to their ears, despite their Buddhist religion, but everything that came out of my mouth was always disappointing and twisted to be anything but truth. I wasn't allowed to ask for things. I learned to stop asking after I found out we were moving to Iowa. I learned to act before asking because I got punished for asking - all I wanted was to be a kid. This was when I really started to become my own person.

I explained all of this to you, Sutton, on our first date when you came over for part two. We stayed up until 5 a.m., talking about our lives. The connection we had was so real and raw. I had never seen anyone be so vulnerable with me as you were. I've always been vulnerable, expressing my feelings since childhood, but I was always told to shut up and never speak my truth. In all my past relationships with friends and men, I had been vulnerable, only for it to be used against me until you came along and saw the real me with no judgment or pity.

The last thing I want is for someone to pity me because of my past struggles. I am a strong, independent woman because I watched the way my mother acted growing up, not having a voice of her own. I made myself a promise when I was 3 or 4 years old that I would never be weak like her. I would never back down on something I believe in. I would never settle for anything less than exceptional. God made me to be great, no matter what others tried to make me believe otherwise.

I've been a fighter my whole life. I fought for everything I had. Nothing was handed to me. I was an illegal alien for a very long time until I turned 18 - that's when it became legal to stay in this country without feeling like I was constantly in darkness. I was in constant fear as my father kept reminding me to watch my P's and Q's and always kiss everyone's asses so we wouldn't get caught being in this country illegally.

I lied to all my friends and teachers about when I came to this country so I could sell the story that I was actually legal. I lied and said I was born here to some, and to others, I said I came to the country when I was five years old to make my story believable - because that's what I was told to do by my father. All the lies I've told about my initial experiences coming to this country got blurry, and I couldn't keep up with my own lies. The guilt consumed me. I always felt so guilty, living in darkness because of the lies I told, but I had no choice but to protect our family's identity. I lied to all my childhood best friends so they would stay my friends. I was ashamed to tell my truth because I desperately wanted to feel accepted.

When I was 16 years old, I finally told the truth to my school counselor regarding my fears and the abuse I endured. I turned my father into the authorities for the physical abuse I experienced because I couldn't take it anymore. The system took me out of my parents' home and put me in a group home until my adopted mother took me in and let me stay with her for nearly a year. She was a blessing from God. She taught me to be strong and accept my parents as they are, understanding that they would never change and that I needed to stop hoping for change that would not happen. She showed me how to be strong and independent, standing on my own two feet.

She said, *"Put your big girl panties on and make something of yourself to show everyone that you can survive anything."* She is no longer with us, but I will forever love her as she gave me the courage to be my own person. My memory is fading as I can't remember her name anymore. The people who read this and know about my past, especially that period, can remind me of one day. The times I stayed with her were inspiring yet terrifying at the same time. I've never felt so free but stuck at the same time.

When I lived with her, I felt safe from my father's wrath, my mother's disappointment in me, and my brother's constant judgment of what a loser I was. But I never felt truly safe. Even though I was safe with my foster mom, I felt fear daily because I couldn't sleep at night - I was deathly terrified of cats. My foster mom had at least ten cats living with us, and they were free to roam the entire house. I wasn't allowed to have the basement door closed where I slept. Waking up with ten cats staring at me was terrifying, as this traumatic feeling brought me back to living in San Francisco with mice and rats running over my body as I slept. My fear of cats started here. Since Gucci and Prada came into my life, my fear and allergy to cats seemed to disappear.

I couldn't complain as I didn't want to show any sign of ungratefulness toward my foster mom - I just remembered her name was Carol. I had nowhere else to go. I couldn't go back to my parents after turning my father in to the authorities; I was afraid he was going to beat me to death if I returned. I've been in survival mode ever since. Every step, every decision I made from then on, was only to survive on my own because I had no options. I've been in survival mode for the rest of my life until my divorce, when I left Dennis Tyler on April 30, 2019. That's when I finally truly felt at peace with myself, able to breathe, no more living in fear of my life, able to be alone independently, and being the strong woman that I was meant to be - until I got sick in February 2020 with brain cancer, also when Dennis passed away on January 2, 2020.

As I explained my life journey to you, Sutton, you explained yours, and we both cried together like we knew each other from a past life. No one in this world understood my pain as no one understood your pain. We understood each other's pain, and that brought us together. We didn't fall in love with our physical beauty, but we fell truly, madly in love with each other's souls that had endured so much pain and trauma together but separately.

On our first date, we were already in love and committed to each other like we had never been in love before. The past pain and suffering in our previous relationships didn't seem to matter anymore because it brought us together in such a most amazing, beautiful, inspiring way. The first night, I dreamt of our entire life together, down to the color of the beach chairs we'd sit on at the beach in Mexico. We envisioned our lives so clearly that I knew from that moment on we had a remarkable story to share with the world through a book I was meant to write from day one. Night after night, my dreams of our lives became more and more real. As you mentioned daily to me how you envisioned the same thing that I had dreamt the night before, I never could understand how you knew that because it was in my dreams the night before. I felt like the Holy Spirit had us dream the same dream every night. Even when you were at Best Western spending time with Bailey, we would dream the same dream. You would tell me what you dreamed about the next day, and it matched my dream exactly.

You envisioned Carter to be the next big artist to write songs about our love and journey; you'd say he would come out with an album for us to dance to on our 50th anniversary. You would dream of how Teagan would run his own company named Harrington's Cleaning and Repair and have Ava and maybe Casey work for him, but you would help manage it until you could not work anymore. You envisioned us living in Florida together after just a week. We made plans and even hired a mover that we had already paid to move. We submitted an application to a place; we were committed to bringing Casey and her sister to live with us, only to motivate Carter to come to Florida in April.

Parts of me wished we should have just taken that leap of faith. After two days of knowing each other, we both called Avery and told her we were getting married. Part of me wished I had taken that leap of faith. Instead, my parents and Avery got inside my head. I knew that disappointed you a lot and made you evaluate if my love for you was real. I completely understand your feeling of doubt in me because of the past relationships you had with women who claimed to love you but abandoned you. I never once wanted you to feel that way about us; I strived every day to assure you that I would never abandon you.

We never fought by yelling like we had in our past relationships. We never got into ugly fights; we always had the respect, love, and understanding for one another, not to say hurtful things that we could not take back. I always choose to walk away, or you choose to walk away. We always came back a couple of hours later and talked it through, becoming closer than we were before. Our disagreements always made us closer, and they were needed for us to grow. Every time we were apart for a couple or few hours, it felt so miserable and daunting. We never felt right being away from each other. We were not meant to be apart.

No one can truly understand the love we shared, but you and I, with God, are always guiding us. We were honest with one another from our first conversation. We had no secrets, even though some truths were very ugly to hear. Our first disagreement was you pulling back because it was Valentine's Day, and you were so overwhelmed as it was the 2-year anniversary of Grandma Barbara's passing. On our first date, you made a promise to take me to Ruth's Chris so you could show me off to everyone that I was your woman. I thought that was the sweetest thing ever - how proud you were to be mine and me to be yours, that you wanted the world to know me, but you didn't want the big bad world to hurt me. A couple of days before Valentine's Day, you got sick and distant from me, and I couldn't understand why. The persistent person that I am, I demanded to know why. You felt pushed and overwhelmed because the love you had for me was too real, and it scared you. It scared you so much that it made you physically sick. I cared so much about your well-being that I offered to bring you Sprite and soup to Extended Stay. Instead, you pushed me away.

I have to admit I was going to give up. After trying to get a hold of you for two days, only for you to be short with me, was enough signs and clues to kick your ass to the curb. One night after, God spoke to me and reminded me of my past relationships, how I easily gave up on men before it got hard and ran from relationships. God reminded me that this was my chance to prove myself and that I could be better. God spoke to me to step up and be the better version of me he knows I can be. He reminded me of the pain I caused others when I gave up on them by not showing enough love and support.

You left clues about where you were that night and where to find you. You left songs and posts on your Facebook to tell me you needed me but were too afraid to show me that I needed to come and rescue you. God put me on this earth to save and rescue people by loving them unconditionally. That's why I've endured so much pain and suffering my entire life - because my mission was to love unconditionally, as I know how it feels to be unloved and unwanted. God spoke to me,

"Don't you give up on this man that I gifted to you."

That night, you moved from Extended Stay to Best Western, and you posted on Facebook with clues. I told you I wasn't going to give up on you and posted that, only for you to block me off your Facebook because you didn't want the people who shot you to know who I was and where I was. I didn't understand that all day. It didn't hit me until that evening what your messages and clues were.

The next night I finally realized this; I took a leap of faith and drove to Extended Stay like a crazy lady, knocking on the door three long times, but no one answered. As I was speaking to God, waiting for you or Teagan to answer the door, no one came, and my heart felt defeated. I sat outside in the hallway, begging God to give me another clue. I felt such disappointment and confusion about the message from God that I cut my losses and walked away. As I was walking outside in the cold, the Holy Spirit carried me a few feet ahead by the wind and said, *"He's not here, you idiot. He's at Best*

Western; remember the post you read yesterday." Then everything clicked.

I rushed over to Best Western, thinking of the one by my place because you had mentioned how great it would be to be within walking distance to me so I didn't have to pick you up because your car needed work, and you didn't have to trouble Teagan with his car. I went to the Best Western on Andover Drive and asked the woman at the counter if she could call Sutton Harrington's room. She said there was no Sutton Harrington there. I asked, *"Are you sure? God told me he was here."* I'm sure, at this point, she thought I was crazy. She then suggested I might want to check the hotel next door, which is also part of Best Western but less pricey - maybe this Sutton of mine was there.

Then I hurried over to Home2 Suites next door, spoke to a gentleman, and asked him to call Sutton Harrington's room or Teagan Harrington's in case you used his name, which wouldn't make sense to me. He said there was no Sutton Harrington, but there was a Sutton Harris. I thought to myself, could you possibly use a different last name to avoid people finding you because of the shooting last year? I questioned this man, *"Are you sure there is no Harrington?"* He said no and asked when you had checked in. I said it should have been that morning. He confirmed that Sutton Harris checked in today after lunch or so. I remembered the post you left after lunch about your cousin blessing you with a room in Best Western that cost less with a hot tub that you always wanted for us to enjoy because that was something you wanted to give me. The guy couldn't give me any more information unless I had gone mad, and I didn't want to get arrested, losing my cool.

I proceeded to walk outside back to my car in the cold, confused once again about the message God left me and your clues, plus the clues the front desk gave me about Sutton Harris supposedly checking in at the same time. After two days of calling you with no response, I said I was going to give up until God spoke to me that night; I felt hopeless because I wasn't going to call you again, only to be ignored. Walking out of Home2 Suites in the cold, again, I felt the Holy Spirit push me to get closer to my car and say, *"Give him a call, you dummy. What the hell are you afraid of?"*

I only called you once the day before and once the day prior, and I texted a couple of times. I left you one message to grab your things at my doorstep as I didn't care to see your face again. I was not going to be labeled as needy or crazy by any man ever again. My thought process was that if you wanted to be in my life, you'd come to me, as I had made that perfectly clear to you from day one that I was not to be played with. So I said to myself, *"Fuck him."* When you never came for your stuff, I decided to throw it in the trash. I said to myself, *"Your damn loss!"* Until everything hit me that night as I was giving up. The Holy Spirit kicked my ass to get in the car and took the chance to call you again.

I was not expecting you to answer. I was expecting that to be my last and final call. It took me by surprise when you did answer. We had a long conversation, or at least I thought we had a long, lucid conversation. At least from my point of view, it was a lucid conversation, but later, I found out your conversation with me was all in your dream, so you thought. I expressed my hurt and the bullshit you pulled, and you kept saying, *"Yes, babe, I promise I'll call you tomorrow after I get off work."* You repeated this repeatedly, at least 15 times, begging me to please trust you and that you loved me and to trust you.

The next day, you called and gave me the most sincere apology with the Twin Flame song that became our song. We talked about all the messages we sent over the last three days and the long conversation I thought I had with you while you were awake and lucid. Only to find out you were dreaming the conversation, that you were not actually awake, but you remembered everything I said and remembered everything you said about how much you loved me and how much you didn't want to lose me; you kept repeating, *"I promise I will call you once I'm off work."*

You also mentioned remembering Teagan telling you all day, *"You're gonna call Joslyn back, right? You promised her, Dad. You better call her,"* as you said to me. You said, *"My own son had to hold me accountable for calling you back because I kept promising and repeating that I would call you back over 15 times."* You said, *"I may be an asshole at times, but I am no liar, and I will never hurt you in that way."*

I then probed a bit more to understand your mental state at that moment. You said you don't remember actually talking to me. All you remembered was Teagan giving you the phone, saying Joslyn was calling, and you answered and carried on a conversation as if you were really talking to me, but somehow you don't remember. Yet, you remembered and retained the content of the conversation.

It was very weird and unbelievable at the same time. Our relationship from day one was weird and unbelievable at the same time. I could never understand how our spirits always connected us, even when we were not physically together. After that night, we both stopped questioning what was weird and unbelievable and just trusted one another. We made a commitment to each other to never give up before things got hard. We promised never to give up, no matter how hard life would get. We promised to love each other for the rest of our lives, and you put that palm leaf you made into a ring, and we got married in my kitchen, naked. After we told

Avery we were to wait all four seasons, you've called me your wifey ever since, but I always called you my white cheddar. It's even on the urn I have for you.

This is what makes us unique and different from any other love story that ever existed. From that moment on, we never questioned our commitment to each other or our love for each other. You stayed with me every night and gave Teagan and Ava the space they needed. You stayed at the hotel only when Bailey cried to have you stay, but sometimes you tried to sneak out to be with me. It was the cutest grandpa thing to do. Your love for him is the most beautiful thing I have ever seen. Bailey was and always will be your world, and I accepted that from day one because that made you the amazing man you are.

That night, we felt free and no longer stuck in our past or anxious about our future. This is when we both decided that February 14th was Grandma Barbara's Day and February 15th would be our Valentine's Day. We didn't make it to our next Valentine's Day, babe, but I will celebrate February 15th with you every year as our Valentine's Day for as long as I live until I see you again. Our love story, so beautifully unconventional, continues to unfold even in your absence. The palm leaf ring you crafted may have withered, but the bond it symbolizes remains unbreakable. I still talk to you, sharing the little moments of my day, imagining your laughter at my jokes, and feeling your comforting presence when times get tough. Teagan and Ava often reminisce about your sneaky *"escape attempts"* from the hotel, chuckling at the memory of you, their lovable grandpa, so smitten that you couldn't bear to be apart. And Bailey, your precious world, carries your spirit in his smile and his kind heart. We share stories about you, keeping your memory alive in every word and every laugh.

Sometimes, I wake up convinced I've had a conversation with you, much like those surreal nights when you dreamed our talks into reality. The line between dreams and wakefulness blurs when it comes to our connection, and I find solace in these moments of closeness, however fleeting they may be.

Our promise to never give up and to love each other for the rest of our lives didn't end with our last breath. It lives on in every choice I make, in every memory I cherish, and in every moment I feel your presence guiding me. You may have left this earthly plane, my White Cheddar, but our love story - weird, unbelievable, and beautiful - continues to write itself in the stars. As I look at your urn, I'm reminded that our love was never about the physical. It was always about the inexplicable connection of our spirits. And that, my love, is something death cannot touch. So I'll keep living, loving, and celebrating us until the day I can sneak out to be with you again, just like you used to do for me.

Chapter 12: A Spiral Chaos

It was a morning like no other. I had to wake up at 3 a.m. this morning to make it to Medina Plastic Surgery by 8 a.m. Sadly, I woke up very late, at nearly 6 a.m. I rushed out the door without putting my contacts in, bringing my glasses and contacts. I drove to Minnesota like a speed demon, going about 95 to 100 miles per hour. I saw five state troopers but luckily didn't get pulled over. I called the doctor's office in the car and informed them of my being late. GPS said I could be there by 10 a.m. Fortunately, the doctor was able to see me even when I arrived late.

I had my consultation done with Dr. Laurence, then rushed over to get my pre-op done at High Point clinic in St. Louis Park. This day had been exhausting and full of anxiety. My heart was thumping from the moment I woke up until I finished my appointments. I felt an overwhelming sense that I couldn't seem to shake.

I received bad news after bad news, first from the doctors and then from my HR department at work. Dr. Laurence mentioned they had to redo the whole surgery for me since the pocket had closed. I had breast implants done nearly 25 years ago, but my left side had ruptured and deflated. The rupture must have happened just before Sutton died, but I didn't realize it until June 18th at Piper's graduation party.

I initially went to a different doctor in Iowa City for a consultation and was led to believe I only had to pay the surgical fees and anesthesia. However, weeks after waiting for the final cost, they quoted me nearly $10,000. That didn't make any sense. This wasn't the first time it ruptured and was under warranty. After weeks of waiting for the final numbers to be not what I was originally told, I had no choice but to go to the doctors in Minnesota, where I had it done before.

After waiting too long, the pocket closed, making the procedure more difficult. I ended up having to pay close to $6,000 instead of $4,000 total. My HR department mentioned that my FMLA forms hadn't reached them to continue the process. Another piece of bad news. Today has been a difficult day, to say the least.

As I was driving back from Minnesota to Iowa City, bad thoughts crossed my mind. I felt very defeated with the day and everything else. At that moment, I felt very hopeless about everything that was happening. I felt the need to check myself into a behavioral health inpatient program where I could get right again. I couldn't get myself checked in just yet as I still had a few things I needed to do.

The following day, I went to the Johnston County courthouse to register the Infinity car from the seller's name to my name. Unfortunately, I couldn't register that day as the bill of sale didn't look clean enough. They needed a new one signed by the seller to register the car. I contacted the seller, but he was out of town and wouldn't be back until July 15th. On July 15th, I was finally able to register the car. That afternoon, I called Faith to come over so she could take me to the emergency room to get myself admitted. She came over and drove me to Mercy Hospital to have myself admitted to the inpatient program. I stayed there for a few hours until they were able to find me a bed at a facility. As I was sleeping, the nurse woke me up and told me I was getting transported to Adel Mental Health Center at 1:30 AM. It was an over two-hour drive.

I felt sick to my stomach when they told me I was being transferred there, not to a hospital nearby. I knew of some people who worked at that hospital, one too close to Adel, Sutton's hometown. When I got there, a friendly nurse made me feel welcome. I was able to go back to bed the moment I arrived.

The next morning, July 16th, I was woken up by a nurse for breakfast. Immediately, I recognized two nurses on the floor as people who knew people Sutton knew. Directly after breakfast, I saw the psychiatrist, who told me she might need me to take new meds. I was told this inpatient program didn't offer any therapy. The whole purpose of checking myself into this kind of place was to get the therapy I needed, not to get more meds in my system.

The doctor said if I didn't want to take more meds, she didn't see the reason why I should stay there. She mentioned I would most likely be discharged on Thursday, 18TH July. I went on with my day, kept my head down, and kept to myself mostly. I got a lot of rest, which is what I wanted. I needed to get my mind and body right again, as I'd been on the go since Sutton died, taking care of everyone else but me. Wednesday, July 17th, rolled around, and I noticed the same two nurses. At this point, I got a bit nervous and maybe paranoid. I spoke up to one of the nurses about the two nurses I recognized and told her my story. I asked to be released that day if possible. After breakfast, I saw the doctor again and was told something completely different. The doctor's demeanor had completely changed. She mentioned to me that my behavior had become erratic and manic all of a sudden. I don't believe my mood or anything had changed whatsoever.

The nurse said I had to take the medication, or she would court order me to take it. Everything she was telling me was completely different from what she had told me the day before. My behavior or mood had remained the same, except I had voiced concern about the two nurses I recognized. At this point, I felt I was being ambushed or retaliated against by the nurses I spoke up about. The social worker, named Jonathan, told me that they could make me take the meds or keep me there longer than I liked.

Thursday, July 18th, rolled around, and I was told that I would not be released, and they didn't know when I would be going home. I had checked myself in voluntarily. I'd kept to myself most of the time and never displayed any manic or erratic behavior that they claimed I had. The facility was surrounded by cameras everywhere. They could pull up all the footage and show me any behavior of that sort. The more I pleaded with them, the more trouble I got into.

This facility did not help me one bit. No therapy was provided, but I was forced to take more medications that I didn't need. In order for me to get out of there, I had to take the medication they wanted me to take. I prayed all day and night to find the best solution for me. I decided to comply and let it all go to God to take care of. On Thursday, July 18th, I decided to take the meds they gave me. The doctor wanted me to take lithium, which is for bipolar disorder. I don't have bipolar disorder, but I was forced to take lithium and olanzapine to help calm my nerves. The new medication made me very sleepy and groggy all the time. They mentioned that even after taking the meds, I would not be guaranteed to leave this place by mid-next week. I continued to pray to God day in and day out. I had to play the cards I was dealt.

I remembered that Sutton had once told me he stayed at this very same hospital about a year ago and was placed in room 307. They placed me in room 307 also. How ironic is that? I played along in their games and activities and behaved as calmly as possible to get released. I had phone calls from Piper, Faith, my brother Hunter, and also Carter while I was there.

Carter made a promise to me that he would put Sutton's ashes in my urn that night or right when I got home. The agreed amount was only the keepsake amount, which is the 3.5 cubic feet size for the keepsake amount. Piper and I had a conversation about why I was really in there in the first place. I explained my frustration with her about Teagan, who was not following through on what he promised about getting a job and not giving me my portion of the ashes that I paid, most of which cost me over 3 thousand dollars. From our last conversation, he had promised through his actions that he was going to do DoorDash. That's the reason why I paid off his violation tickets of $475. He made a promise that it wouldn't only be a verbal promise, that he would show through his actions that he would get a job. Those promises were only words. He never once followed through on his word. I explained to Piper my frustration with the amount of money I'd spent on Teagan, Carter, Ava, and Casey, but I still hoped they would get better. I also explained my paranoia about staying in that hospital. The more I explained things to Piper, the more she thought I was too paranoid.

Days went by, and I kept my head down and did what I was told. Finally, on July 21st, a Sunday, the doctor said I was going to be released on July 22nd. Monday came around, and I waited to be released. Hunter picked me up at close to 5 pm. I heard the news from Piper that she, Teagan, and Carter all had some words that weren't very pleasant.

I texted Carter on my way back home from the hospital to ask if he was home so I could get into the apartment. He replied that he was with his mom in Adel, having dinner. I then texted Piper to ask if she had my other spare key so I could get into my apartment. She responded that she was at work and

Carter should be home, or the key should be in the apartment. Piper said she would ask Carter. A minute later, she gave me a screenshot of the conversation she had with Carter about the key. He mentioned he didn't have the key to the apartment. For the past five weeks, Carter and Casey have been living with me on the sectional, and he had access to my apartment as he had the key. That is why I was inquiring about the key when I got released from the hospital.

At this point, I got nervous as to why he didn't have a key to the apartment, as he should have had one copy since he lived with me. One of his text messages said not to disturb him as he was having dinner with his mom in Adel. At this point, I just wanted my key to get into my apartment. I stopped over at Piper's work to pick up the spare key.

I came home and noticed all of Carter's and Casey's belongings were gone except for a few things. Carter even left his shoes that I bought on my bed. My mind was racing to all sorts of situations that could possibly happen. I wondered if he had moved out. I saw his guitars and other equipment were not taken. I texted Casey to find out where they were. She responded that they were at Chuck E. Cheese in town on the 42nd, celebrating Bailey's birthday. I asked if they were coming back. She explained that they had an altercation with Piper and I should blame Piper for why they no longer lived with me.

According to Piper, she spoke to Teagan about getting a job and paying me back for the money he owed me. Teagan ended up hanging up on her during that conversation, which led nowhere. Then I wondered what that had to do with Carter and Casey. Casey explained that Piper was yelling at Carter on top of that, disrespecting him, and said that I didn't want them to live with me anymore. I called Piper to find out the whole story. She mentioned that she spoke to Carter about Teagan. Carter went off on her about how she spoke to him and told her to leave him out of it. Carter mentioned he just wanted to be left out of it. Piper said okay, but he yelled at her about how she spoke to him. I asked Casey why Carter hadn't stayed out of it. I mentioned to Casey that this kind of altercation had happened before when Carter stuck his nose where it didn't belong. This whole thing was only toward Teagan, not Carter.

When Carter decided to get in the middle, even after he said he wanted to stay out of it, he still intruded on the conversation. I myself have had these talks with Carter before where he needs to stop enabling his brother for not getting a job. Carter gets hot-headed and tends to talk without thinking, which puts him in a world of trouble. I asked Casey if we all could sit together that night to discuss this calmly. She said she would ask Carter, but nothing was definite. I asked what was going on now moving forward. Carter said I should thank Piper for everything, especially how everything had blown up, and that she needed to apologize to him.

I asked about the ashes and when I could get my portion. I texted Teagan and Ava, but there was no response. Casey responded that I could get my portion when I got a small urn that fits the ashes. I mentioned that I paid over $3,128 for the ashes and agreed to get my portion a couple of times prior but never followed through, and I was promised by Carter just two days ago that he would pour it into my urn when I got home. Casey responded that this was all I was going to get and that I should feel lucky that I got what I already had in my necklace, as all the women only got that. I asked her to explain what she meant by that. She said the boys would only allow me to have my portion if I got another small urn, as they didn't like the urn I had already. I responded by asking why that matters and what kind of urn I got. I asked her, isn't it that they are trying to control me in this aspect? She said she didn't care and I only needed to comply with their wishes.

I reminded her again that he had promised me just two days ago, not to mention that the initial promise was to split evenly by four for Teagan, Jacob, Carter, and me. Casey mentioned that I only took care of them by providing them with food and all the necessities, plus concert tickets, shoes, music equipment, a car, and vacation, only to get ashes. I said I paid for that, too. Casey confirmed to me in a text that they never intended to give me any ashes in the first place. They just took my money, knowing that I would provide to pay for the ashes and everything else.

This was when I realized I got played by Sutton's sons, both Teagan and Carter and their girlfriends. I texted Carter to find out what was going to happen to the San Diego vacation that was already paid for. He said he wasn't going, and the rest weren't going either until Piper gave him a heartfelt apology, which she had already done that morning before I got released from the hospital. I mentioned this to Casey, but she said that the apology didn't happen and it was a joke. I sent the screenshot of the apology to Casey and asked her if this wasn't an apology and a heartfelt one. Then what would you call that? She continued her nasty attitude towards it and said to me, bottom line, I would not get Sutton's ashes.

I told her it was not a smart idea to cross me after all I had done to help her. Casey texted me, saying all the accusations Piper made were what I wanted. Things were misinterpreted from the beginning. That's why I wanted to have a calm conversation until Casey made it messy. Carter told me to leave Casey alone. I asked him why he doesn't fight his battles and not have his girlfriend do it. I asked

Carter to have enough balls to face me and talk to me.

At the same time, Teagan responded to me, telling me the exact same thing - that Piper was disrespectful to him. Ava texted me the same, too. I didn't hear back from any of them that night. Piper gave another heartfelt apology again, but I didn't hear anything back from anyone. Piper only apologized for being the bigger person; she wasn't in the wrong for the things she said to Teagan.

The next morning, I got a Facebook message from June Calhoun. I knew that message would be another nasty message I had received from her three times before. I texted Carter and Teagan, both asking why they sent their mother to me regarding this matter. I asked them both to have enough balls to deal with this on their own. I told Carter that if he or Teagan insisted that I deal with their mom on this matter, then she would be welcome to come to me and that I would offer her lemonade or tea. Carter responded, saying, *"Ain't nobody has anyone text you should have listened to my dad when he told me you were crazy," "Enjoy your ashes and thank Piper and try some shit. You took me to a dispensary and supplied weed to minors."* Carter made threats and false accusations. He said he didn't run to his mom. He said I was being fake to him, Carter, Teagan, and Ava this whole time. He mentioned he would be over to get the rest of his things. He wanted all the things he left here, from the guitars to the speakers I paid for, among other things.

I said to him I would not return any of his stuff until he gave me my portion of the ashes he promised. He refused and said he would come and get the guitar from me if he wanted to, and I couldn't stop him. He also mentioned that he had taken some video of me walking out of a dispensary in Kansas City from the beginning, and he knew he had to do that as leverage as he couldn't trust me from the beginning. I thought to myself, if that was true, that they didn't trust me from the beginning, then why did they trust taking my money, food, hospitality, home, and a car I bought so they could get a job and vacation, among other things?

Later that day, Casey's mom, Sage Terry, decided to message me and say I needed to return the guitars to Carter as Sutton bought them. She mentioned if I returned both guitars, maybe Carter would give me the ashes. For one of the guitars, Sutton bought the electric white guitar, but for the other guitar, I paid over $220, so it's not his guitar. She proceeded to keep messaging me after I told her to stay in her lane. Then she proceeded to continue the conversation, and it got ugly. I warned her to stop, but she kept going. I ended up blocking her.

This is when everything finally sank in for me - that they were only around to use me for my money. But they turned around and said Sutton only used me for my money and that he was cheating on me the entire time. These are the words of Sutton's son, Teagan Harrington. He said Sutton was having sex with Sage Terry that night when I came to his hotel room looking for him. I knew better because Sutton didn't have a working car, and Sage didn't have a car or a license, plus she lives in the Decorah area. I knew at this point Teagan and Carter would do anything and say anything to hurt me and especially to put doubts in my head about the love their father had for me so they could break me.

I contacted the Iowa City police and explained my situation to them about wanting to exchange guitars for ashes. I was told by the police they could contact them, but they could not ask for the ashes as that is a civil matter. About an hour later, the police knocked on my door to give me back my key to the apartment and the key to my car that I bought for Teagan and Ava to use. In exchange, they wanted both guitars. I asked for my ashes; they said no. I said I could return one guitar that Sutton paid for and the other guitar I was keeping as I paid for that.

The police asked to see the title of the car; I showed him that the car belonged to me, not Teagan. Carter asked for his birth certificate and Casey's driver's license. I explained to the police that I didn't have his birth certificate; he had it last when he was filling out his orientation paperwork for McDonald's when he was hired. I wouldn't have Casey's driver's license. She had just got her driver's test two weeks prior, and the license had not come in the mail yet. I opened my mailbox and showed the officer it wasn't there. I let the officers look around my apartment if they were not satisfied. They looked around a bit and found nothing. I even let them look in my car for any birth certificate where he thought he had it last. Nothing was found. The police mentioned that if there were any more items that needed to be returned to me, I would have to file a civil court case as they would not deal with this anymore.

On July 24th, I decided to talk to the landlord of the Cascade apartments where Teagan was living. I had gotten that apartment for him under my name as primary. After all the threats he made and the lies he told me about Sutton, I knew there was nothing left to salvage our relationship. I wanted him out of my life for good before Carter decided to trash that apartment like he trashed Sutton's apartment 2 years ago in Cambrian, cost Sutton over $24,000 and put him in debt.

I talked to Jason, the landlord. We agreed that in order to get out of the lease, both Teagan and I had to write a letter saying we wanted to vacate. At this point, I knew he wasn't going to do that for me. Jason came up with a plan to ask him to provide proof of income that he could afford to live there without my income or my name. Jason gave the notice to Teagan regarding the apartment and gave him five days to come up with proof of income, showing he had a job or was hired at a job and showing a job hire letter.

The next day, on the 25th, I was told by my best friend Sanvi that Ava's dad called him asking about what I was doing about their apartment living situation. Apparently, Dustin, who is Ava's dad, was worried that she would be homeless. I texted Ava and told her not to have her dad text my friends asking about her living situation anymore. I told her to have Teagan talk to me if he was concerned about his living situation and to stop having her fight his battles for him.

Ava responded, saying she never thought I would do that to her. I explained to her that I wasn't doing this. I told her to stop enabling Teagan. He needed to get a job and make his own money in order to save himself. He needed to stop being a bum, staying home, smoking weed and playing video games all day and night. He needed to provide for his son and her. I told her I would help her if he could talk to me and show remorse for what he said to me and kick Carter and Casey out of the apartment as they were living there after they both chose to leave my apartment. The apartment only occupied two adults and a minor child; they were not allowed to be in there. She refused to kick them out. I said I couldn't help her.

The next morning, she texted, saying they were both out of the apartment. I advised her to talk to Jason, the landlord. I also mentioned I had a gift for Bailey for his birthday. I never got a response back from Ava until I was already in San Diego. Before I left for San Diego, I had to have a session with my attending psychiatrist, who took me off the lithium and did not understand why the doctors at that hospital made me take those medications that I clearly did not need as I don't show signs of any bipolar. The Olanzapine did help me sleep better at night, so he recommended I stay on that so I could stop taking the gummies at night.

Chapter 13: Chaos Follows Me to San Diego

I texted Teagan and Ava to find out about the August 14th celebration of life that was already planned for you at 11 am at Valley Church. No responses from either of them. I'd already ordered the small keepsake urn that Casey told me I had to order, but it doesn't come overnight. The estimated delivery time was July 26 to August 3.

This morning, I got a notification saying that the urn I ordered should be in my mailbox tonight by 8 pm. I messaged Teagan and Ava again but have still not received a response. I spoke to your mom, Diane, and she told me she would reach out to Teagan and try to plead with him to give me the ashes. The whole point of going to San Diego tomorrow was to spread your ashes.

Later that afternoon, after running errands around town, I got home to see a package at my door. Surprise! The urn got to me early, at 2:30 pm. I messaged your mom and told her it was here. I sent a picture of the urn to Ava to let her know. Later that evening, your mom confirmed that Teagan would only give me my portion of the urn at 3.5 cubic feet if I stayed outside the apartment. I asked your mom, *"How do I know for sure he's going to fill it with your real ashes and not some dirt?"* She said she'd have him video it for her as he's filling it out. I trust your mom, so I agreed. I arrived at Teagan's apartment with my brother Hunter. He opened the door, and I gave him a small urn to fill up while I waited outside. Minutes later, he came back with the filled urn. I told him then that I wanted to get the Apple iPhone back since he hadn't paid his phone bill since May, and it was missed for June and July. He said okay and agreed to return it once he had time to transfer the data.

This phone plan we got together when you were still alive on April 15, it was agreed he was to pay his phone bill on time every month. He only paid for May 5, just a day before you died. After you left us, he decided to stop showing up to work altogether and didn't feel the need ever to go back to work to help himself as I was taking care of the bills and all he needed. I guess going back to work was pointless to him when I was already providing everything he needed. Teagan did apologize for the way things went down a few days ago. All I said to him was, *"The things you said to me were extremely hurtful,"* and I left it at that. He has apologized in the past for his outburst but is never truly sorry for his actions to make a change.

Tomorrow was the trip to San Diego. Avery got a promotion from her job, so she couldn't make it as she had to work with no one covering the management shifts. Carter, Casey, Teagan, Ava, and Bailey can't make it either due to the confrontation over the last few days. My eyes are wide open now, to say the least, about what these kids are capable of. Jacob, Ashley, Taylor, Jada, and Caleb were all able to make it at least, plus Piper and Valerie on a different flight. I was able to get everything packed up in 15 minutes. Got our apartment cleaned up and everything ready for me to fly out in the morning. It was agreed that Piper and I would carpool together to MN at the same time as my flight leaves at 10 am, and her flight leaves just the next day out of MN airport. She was planning on staying at Valerie's house in MN the night prior, anyway.

Piper picked me up at 5 am to drive to MN. She dropped me off at Terminal 1 for the Delta flight. I'd already checked in online. No bags to check. I was ready for the TSA line. While waiting in the TSA line, I put up a post on my Facebook page (as I always post publicly), saying, *"Flying out alone to San Diego to spread Sutton's ashes. The others chose to be little shits, and Avery had to miss the trip due to work. Meeting the rest on a later flight. We will make the best of what we have."* I Got several likes and comments such as *"have fun,"* etc.

I boarded the flight and turned off my phone for silence and peace. Arrived in San Diego at 2:45 PM, turned my phone on, and got a notification from Sunny Tyler. I wondered, who the heck is Sunny Tyler? Her comment stated, *"Okay, Joslyn, I thought you didn't have any of his ashes. That's why you're pissed off at the kids, so my question is, did you sneak some out of the urn without them knowing? Help me understand what's going on here because aren't you supposed to be the adult just saying."* I was waiting in line to get off the plane.

While reading this comment, Sunny Tyler left me. I thought to myself, who the heck is she and how do I know her? Why the heck is it any of her business regarding Sutton's ashes? Also, who does she think she is to accuse me of stealing Sutton's ashes? I replied to her comment, saying, *"Teagan gave me some last night. You should communicate with him. I gave back the guitar and the shoes as agreed, even though Carter still had more of my things. Also, I'm not a thief. I don't need to sneak anything even though I have the key to the apartment. I don't operate in a sneaky manner. That's not my style."* Sunny replied, *"It was very nice of him to do that for you. I will apologize for my comment about his ashes, but please don't call my grandchildren out of their names. You played a part in the situation."* I responded, saying, *"You comment on my post. If you don't want to be called out publicly, don't publicly raise the topic in my post. You should've PM me. Is that a thought? Hmmm."*

Sunny commented back, *"Okay, now I will end this conversation because I really am trying to be the bigger person here, and if you knew anything about me, you know how hard that is for me. I really don't know you, and you definitely don't know me, so we'll leave it at that. We only have one thing in common: you were a part of Sutton's life, and Sutton was a part of mine. His children and my grandchildren have lived together. That is how we blended, so you carry on with your plans. I know how important it is to follow through on something that you had told someone that you loved who has passed away. I did that last year for my best friend, who also passed away."* At this point, the conversation went on for a long time. I wanted this conversation to end quickly, but it went on till the next day. I commented back, saying, *"Good to know you respect my page, and I respect you. It's a two-way street. You were the one who made accusations that I sneak ashes without permission; wasn't that what I read in plain English? Who's being the bigger person here? And how old are you? So please, you wanna be the bigger person, just back off before I tear you apart. That's me being the bigger person. I'm nice till I'm pushed, then I am a real bitch. That's all you need to know, and your grandkids learned that the hard way. So please stay off my page unless you want me to start a war on yours. Didn't think so. Also, stop acting like they are really your grandkids. Just the whole Decorah town acting like y'all everyone's mamas but can't support the kids financially but can claim they're your kids. I'm the one who has been supporting them for the last two and a half months. SMH."*

The comments and accusations still kept coming in till the next day. Nasty words were exchanged, and lies were told about how Sutton never loved me. In fact, he was hooking up with her daughter Sage Terry the whole time I was in a relationship with Sutton. She made more accusations, and the rest of her friends in Decorah also jumped into the conversation because I blocked Sunny Tyler. Another girl, her friend named Annie Richards, commented, but only to find out it was Sunny using her account to comment, saying more lies and nasty things. I then blocked her. I didn't come to San Diego to deal with these women. I mentioned in my post that I would file harassment charges if they didn't stop. Once I blocked both of them, the comments stopped. After I arrived in San Diego, I got news from Ashley that their flight was delayed. Then I got word they were boarding 2 hours later. Another bad news was that they had to evacuate the plane as the engine broke down. They had to get a new plane to fly to San Diego. I had rented two car rentals at that time, knowing another driver would arrive on time to pick up the car. That car rental ended up being canceled because the plane arrived later than expected. I ordered another car rental to pick up at 11 pm when I thought they'd board the plane initially, but only to find out they had to evacuate the plane due to engine issues. I have to cancel that car rental now, too. I'd already paid for both car rentals at this point. I was really frustrated at all this chaos.

I got a message from Ashley that they were going to board the plane at 7:30 pm. Which means they wouldn't arrive till about midnight. After dealing with the nasty comments from Sunny Tyler and the car rental issues, my day was already a disaster. I barely had time to get dinner before I had to pick them up from the airport. Due to traffic in San Diego, it takes 40 minutes to get to the airport and 45 minutes to get back from the airport to the Wyndham Club Center, where my home timeshare is located. We stopped and got food for Ashley, Jacob, and all the kids. We didn't get back till 2:30 AM. We finally got a good night's sleep.

The next morning, Piper awakened me at 6 am, saying she was leaving for her flight. Her and Valerie's flight was supposed to get in at close to 11 am San Diego time. It took me over 45 minutes to get to the airport and another hour to find them. After I was able to find them, we had to rush over to another rental car company to pick up another car since it was too late to pick one up for Ashley to drive last night. After everything was done, it was already 3 in the afternoon, and most of our day had already passed by.

We stayed at the resort and just enjoyed the amenities the resort had to offer on the 1st day. That was already a Sunday; I had already been in San Diego from the day before on Saturday from 2:45 pm. I haven't accomplished any relaxation time yet. We got back to the resort, gave one car to Ashley to drive, and then we all headed over to the grocery store to stock up on food, but the weather decided to rain on us for a few hours. There goes pool day. We all decided to go gift shopping instead. They all brought something to take back home for family and friends. We got back to the resort, and the pool was already closed.

Chapter 14: Magic, Memories, and Mayhem

After a good night's sleep, Monday finally arrived. We agreed that this would be our Disneyland Park day, as the weather forecast looked promising. I woke up a bit later than intended, only to discover that Ashley, Jacob, and the kids had already made their way to Disneyland Park. However, they faced an unexpected hurdle – the ticket prices were higher than initially anticipated, preventing them from entering the park.

Without hesitation, I assured them I'd cover the difference. Hurrying out of bed, I quickly purchased all the tickets and rushed to meet them at the gate. Upon arrival, we encountered another setback. Ashley and Jada's outfits didn't meet the park's dress code. Thinking on their feet, they suggested I dashed to one of the nearby stores to buy a couple of suitable shorts for them to wear inside the park.

By the time we finally made it through the gates, it was already 2:30 in the afternoon. Our stomachs growled in unison, so we prioritized lunch before embarking on our Disney adventure.

The rest of the day at Disneyland was filled with excitement and joy. We rode various attractions, savored the park's unique cuisines, and capped off the night with a spectacular fireworks display at the Cinderella Castle at 10 pm. As I sat there, enveloped by the enchanting music and dazzling pyrotechnics, a wave of melancholy washed over me. I couldn't help but wish you were there with us, Sutton. My mind drifted to all the times we shared and the numerous places we'd talked about visiting together. This Disneyland Park was one of those destinations we'd dreamed of experiencing as a couple. Throughout the 30-45 minute fireworks show, I imagined you sitting beside me. Tears of sadness streamed down my face as the harsh reality hit me once again – I would never see you again, and we'd never get to share moments like these or visit all the places we'd dreamed about together.

In the midst of my emotional turmoil, Caleb wrapped me in a big hug. Glancing behind me, I noticed Jacob, his eyes glistening with light tears. I knew at that moment he was thinking about you too. The weight of our loss felt palpable – it was as if the time we should have had with you had been cruelly snatched away from us.

The following day, we ventured to Six Flags. We enjoyed a few rides before the weather turned on us again. It seemed that rain had become an unwelcome companion on this trip, making frequent appearances. I hadn't realized that it would rain this much in San Diego. Every day, without fail, it would pour for hours, typically from the afternoon well into the evening. I did my research, and it shows that July was not the rainy season in San Diego.

Wednesday, July 31st, finally brought us the best weather we'd seen since our arrival. Seizing the opportunity, we decided to spend the day at Mission Beach. We arrived early, allowing us to bask in the sun and play in the sand for the entire day. I had previously agreed to meet my friend Sage Patterson, who lives in Los Angeles, and I was planning to drive there and meet her by 7:30 PM. However, I had grossly underestimated the traffic and the distance. Even with good road conditions, the drive from Mission Beach to Los Angeles would take a solid two hours.

Realizing the impracticality of our original plan, we decided to postpone our Los Angeles visit to the next day, Thursday, when we were scheduled to visit SeaWorld. Ashley, Jacob, and the kids opted to leave the beach earlier, around 5 pm. As I was packing up our beach gear, Piper expressed her desire for an early dinner. I suggested we dine at *"Coconuts on the Beach,"* a charming beachside restaurant.

The meal was delightful – I savored the absolutely delicious conch fritters. Piper opted for the chicken alfredo, while Valerie enjoyed some buffalo chicken wings. Both girls indulged in mango smoothies, which I also found incredibly refreshing.

The next day, we set our sights on Sea World. For some reason, I had mistakenly believed SeaWorld was in Los Angeles, but I soon realized it was actually in San Diego. Unfortunately, Caleb had fallen ill the night before, so Ashley and Jacob stayed behind at the resort with him. I took Jada and Taylor with us to the park, where we marveled at the killer whale show, much to their delight. We also enjoyed a few rides and had lunch at the park.

Later in the day, we received a call from Ashley informing us that Caleb was feeling better. We met them at the gate to hand over their tickets so they could join us. The rest of the day was filled with fun as we explored the park together. We were captivated by the dolphin show and spent time observing the stingrays. The kids couldn't resist picking up some toys from the gift shop before we all sat down for dinner at one of the park's restaurants.

As if on cue, the sky opened up again while we were having dinner. The rain persisted until 9 pm that night, making locating our cars in the downpour challenging. Between the relentless rain and heavy traffic, our GPS indicated it would take us two hours to reach Los Angeles from SeaWorld. It took us an entire hour to exit the SeaWorld parking lot.

The constant rain in San Diego had begun to take its toll, leaving me feeling utterly exhausted. While we had enjoyed one good day at SeaWorld and another at the beach, I couldn't help but reflect on how this trip had turned into quite an ordeal. From the hurtful comments made by the ladies in Decorah, Iowa, to the flight delays, engine issues, car rental problems, the persistent traffic, Caleb falling ill, and the daily deluges – it truly felt like a perfect storm of disasters. I made a mental note to myself: never visit San Diego in July again. Maybe it was just my bad luck this time around. Due to the combination of heavy traffic and rain, it took us three and a half hours to get back to our resort from SeaWorld. Regretfully, I had to cancel our meeting with Sage Patterson as Piper had fallen ill from all the rain exposure. Moreover, with traffic at a standstill, it was already 6 pm by the time we left the parking lot, and it would have taken another three hours to reach Los Angeles. My initial plan was to visit Sage briefly during our stay, but she worked until 4 pm daily, leaving little room for a meet-up. Unfortunately, we didn't get the chance to see her this time around.

Upon returning to the resort, we prepared for a poignant ceremony we had planned – the release of paper lanterns into the sky. I had purchased these lanterns and had them delivered to the resort earlier. We took time to inscribe the names of all the people you loved on these lanterns. The first lantern bore the names of Teagan, Carter, Ava, and Bailey.

The second was dedicated to Jacob, Ashley, Caleb and their children. My name and Piper's graced the third lantern. Your brothers Joseph and Duane, along with the outlaw and your mom (affectionately referred to as Mama Bear), were honored on the fourth lantern. The fifth and final lantern was reserved for your three best friends, whom you had often spoken about with such fondness – Tory Highland, Dimitri, and Whiley.

We released the lanterns one by one into the night sky, capturing each moment on video to share with your mom later. Following this touching tribute, I spread your ashes into the lake near a gazebo surrounded by live butterflies. In an almost surreal moment, a large swan approached me just after I had scattered your ashes. We all shared a nervous chuckle, jokingly hoping the swan wouldn't consume your ashes. *"Let's hope that swans don't eat your ashes and, well, you know,"* I said, addressing God with a mix of humor and reverence. After this meaningful night of remembrance, lantern releases, and the spreading of your ashes, we called it a day, our hearts heavy but full.

Friday morning arrived, signaling departure day for Piper and Valerie. Given the horrendous traffic we'd encountered over the past few days, they wisely opted to reach the airport three hours early. I managed to catch some sun that morning while Jacob, Ashley, and the kids, all of whom had fallen ill by this point, stayed in for most of the day, only venturing out to the pool for a couple of hours. After dropping Piper and Valerie at the airport, I made it back to the resort by 3 in the afternoon.

True to form, the rain made its appearance yet again, pouring for several hours and thwarting our plans to visit the water park. The downpour persisted until after 6:30 pm. With this being our last night at the resort, I suggested we all go out for dinner. We chose the ICHIBAN buffet on W Lake Broman Rd in San Diego, California. Unfortunately, the others barely touched their food, still feeling under the weather from the previous day's events. We finished our meal and called it a night, ready to put this challenging day behind us.

The next morning, Jacob and Ashley informed me that Carter had reached out to her, questioning why Casey's name wasn't included on the paper lanterns. Ashley redirected him to me, explaining she wasn't privy to those decisions. Jacob became visibly upset, sharing that Casey had apparently received some of your ashes. Confused, I asked how he knew this. He explained that based on what Teagan was saying, it seemed Casey had been given a portion of your ashes.

Jacob's distress was palpable, struggling to understand why Casey, who wasn't family, would receive your ashes. I responded, confirming that she wasn't family and that you didn't like her. I recounted how, from our first date, you had expressed your dislike for her, only tolerating her presence for your son, Carter, whom you often described as ungrateful and uncontrollable. I even reminded Jacob about how you had initially tried to set Carter up with my daughter Piper during our first date – an idea I quickly shut down due to its potential awkwardness.

For months, I tried to calm your concerns about Casey, even defending her. You consistently maintained that she had a nasty attitude and wished Carter would end their relationship. I realized now that I should have listened to you more closely. You were right all along. The night I returned home from the Adel Mental Health Center, I finally saw Casey Ronald's true colors. She viciously lashed out at me, claiming I should be grateful for the small amount of your ashes I had in a necklace, insisting I didn't deserve any, according to her. Seeing Jacob so distraught about being left out of receiving his father's ashes while Casey, a non-family member, had been given some deeply upset me. I attempted to reach out to Teagan about this matter, but as expected, my messages went unanswered. I suspected he had already blocked me, conveniently forgetting that I was paying for the phone he was using to communicate.

Just two days prior, on July 31st at 2:12 A.M., I was jolted awake by two phone calls from Ava and two text messages claiming their roof was caving in and they needed my help. When I finally answered, it was Teagan on the line, insisting that their roof was leaking badly and on the verge of collapse. I asked why he hadn't called maintenance, to which he replied that he had, but no one had picked up. I advised him to keep calling and leave messages. He sent me a picture of the ceiling showing some water drips, but it didn't appear to be substantial. He also shared an image of his skylight illuminated by lightning.

I reminded him that it was almost 3 in the morning, and there wasn't much I could do from San Diego. I suggested he wait for maintenance to return his call. I suspect this response further agitated Teagan as I went back to sleep, reiterating that I could do nothing from my current location.

The day before leaving for San Diego, Teagan and Ava sought my help to prevent their eviction by their landlord despite the harsh words and lies Teagan had previously directed at me. He had attempted to apologize after I retrieved your ashes from him the night before, indicating he was aware of the hurt he had caused. However, I didn't entertain his apology, simply stating, *"You really hurt me with the words you said."* I left it at that. I believe his feelings were hurt again because I didn't forgive him, and when he called in the early hours about the roof issue, I didn't indulge that either. This seems to have provoked him to retaliate by informing Jacob that Casey had received some of your ashes. I only learned about Casey getting ashes through Jacob that Friday morning.

In response to this situation, I made a public post explaining why Casey's name was not included on the paper lanterns. I also took the opportunity to shed light on the questionable characters associated with Casey, including her mother, Sage Terry, whom I described as a drug dealer who had attempted to have you sell her drugs through the Humpty Dumpty bar. Sage Terry commented on my post, which I promptly deleted, leading to an exchange of harsh words before she decided to block me. I had intentionally unblocked her on Facebook prior to making this post, knowing her curiosity (or that of her associates in Decorah, IA) would lead her to see it.

As anticipated, the comments began pouring in, creating the public drama I had hoped to provoke. More lies and false accusations about you emerged. It seemed everyone from Decorah, including women who worked at the Stop and Go gas station, had something to say. They spread malicious lies, claiming you wanted to sleep with Piper, and that was the real reason I ended our relationship. They portrayed you as a terrible Padfield and insinuated that you only got together with me to use me for my money. I knew better than to believe their lies. After multiple attempts to ask them to leave my post, they persisted. I responded by questioning their claims of love and care for you, asking why they were tarnishing your good name. I called them out for continuing to provide you with free alcohol, suggesting that was the real reason you frequented the gas station – because all the women there were infatuated with you and gave you free food and liquor.

I pointed out that giving away free food and alcohol is essentially stealing from their employers. I hinted to them that maybe you were only using them all along, but you finally found your true love with me and were actually honest and sincere with me because I didn't have to give you free food or alcohol to love me. I did not have to buy your love. You may have been the kind of man they know, but the man I know is a new and improved version of you who is honest and loving. That side of you that no one knows besides me and God.

Eventually, after I repeatedly mentioned filing harassment charges, they stopped. Upon returning from San Diego the next day, I reported the incident to the police. The officer who took my statement and police report informed me that they had reached out to the individuals involved, warning them to cease their behavior or face potential harassment charges. As a precaution, I took screenshots of all the comments in case they decided to delete them.

Threats had been made against me. Carter had stated that if they wanted to retrieve their belongings, they would do so regardless of what I said. Sunny Tyler had threatened that she didn't care about me and could make her point to me anytime she wanted. Sage Terry had menacingly said she couldn't wait to see me and observe my reaction. These people knew where I lived. In response, I boldly stated, *"Okay, bring it on. I'm ready. I'll be home at 7:30 PM on August 3rd. I'm prepared for you."*

I arrived home a bit earlier than stated and waited outside my apartment, ready for any confrontation. No one showed up. In light of this, I decided to make another public post, stating that if anything were to happen to me and it was ruled a suicide, it should not be believed. I emphasized that I would never take my own life, especially not by gunshot, just as you would never have done so unless you were under the influence of drugs or had something slipped in your drink.

My post went on to question the circumstances surrounding your death. I expressed my belief that you didn't simply take your own life because you were intoxicated that night, suggesting that something else had occurred – something that Carter, Casey, and Demonte weren't revealing. I brought up the fact that the gun belonged to Mary Jane, who initially claimed it was stolen before changing her story to say it was given to you later in the investigation.

I pointed out that the investigation was closed as a suicide based solely on the testimony of young individuals who were abusing alcohol and drugs. I revealed that the house where you died was known to be full of fentanyl and meth, information that came directly from Carter. He had mentioned to me that he didn't need to get a job, as he could survive by selling drugs in Decorah as he had done in the past. I emphasized that this was something you would never have approved of, and I was certain there had been some altercation on the night you supposedly shot yourself.

Your mom and I had pieced together much of what happened that night, and the timeline didn't add up. She mentioned that you had messaged Carter at 4 pm, asking if everything in the house was okay. This struck me as odd – why would you ask that unless something wasn't right? What had transpired in the house that prompted you to leave and send such a text?

I recalled receiving a text from you around 3 pm saying, *"Yeah, well, I need to spend some time with Carter and get his house straight. He has some issues with electricity and shit. I'm gonna stay with him for a minute and get his shit right since Teagan is Gucci right now."* When I asked about our plans to grill ribs that night, you responded, *"Give it to Teagan for tonight. I'll be home tomorrow."*

None of it made sense. You seemed to be in a good mood, even according to your friend Chester Holland in Decorah, who had heard from others who saw you that night that you were in high spirits after returning from the bar. But supposedly, after getting back to the Decorah house belonging to Sage Terry, where Carter, Casey and Demonte had been living, you shot yourself the moment you got home. According to the police scanner, Demonte made a statement to the police: *"My neighbor Sutton Harris got in an argument with my sister and came out and shot himself."* This statement puzzled me because Demonte knew you were Carter's dad and that Casey was dating Carter. He knew you and Carter well enough to know that you weren't his neighbor and that your last name wasn't Harris.

It finally dawned on me that Demonte was deflecting, trying to distance himself from you in the eyes of the police. If it was truly a suicide, why did he need to pretend he didn't know you well enough to know your real last name or that you actually lived in that house? Why lie to the cops and say you were a neighbor when they all lived in the same house? None of it added up.

I became convinced that Demonte and Casey were somehow involved in your death. I suspected that some drug-related dispute had occurred in that house, leading to an argument or altercation between Demonte and Casey. Carter had told the police that you had too much to drink, so he told you to leave the house, and that's when you supposedly shot yourself. But according to Demonte, it was an argument with Casey. The stories were full of holes, and I was determined to uncover the truth, no matter how painful it might be.

Chapter 15: Finding Justice While I Put You to Rest

The days following my return from San Diego were far from the calm I had hoped for. Instead, they were filled with a whirlwind of emotions, tasks, and an ever-growing suspicion that your death wasn't what it seemed. The celebration of life I had planned for August 14, 2024, became a point of contention, with your sons Teagan and Carter trying to put a stop to it. But I couldn't let their feelings, however hurt they might be, prevent us from honoring your memory.

When the church coordinator called to inform me that Teagan didn't want the service at Valley Church, I felt a surge of determination. You had been gone for over three months, and we needed to have a service in a timely manner. I wasn't about to let anyone, even your own son, ruin that day for you. So, I decided to proceed with a private service, even without their blessing.

The conflict extended beyond just the service. Your uncle said he would only show up if I returned Carter's things - a small speaker and a gaming headset he'd left at my place. He'd also taken the laptop I bought for his schooling and another item I'd loaned him. I told your uncle I'd return the speaker and headset only if my belongings were returned. His threats to cause trouble at the service only steeled my resolve. On that day, Pastor Bolan performed a beautiful ceremony. My friends from Avery, Fatih, Saavi, Piper, and my family all showed up. Even your childhood best friend, Ben Miller, made an appearance. The absence of your boys was palpable, but their hatred for me seemed to outweigh their love for you. It broke my heart, but I couldn't dwell on it. The flowers arrived at the church, a stunning arrangement of white and purple, just as you would have liked.

After the service, we gathered for a small reception, sharing stories about you over pulled pork and other comfort foods. Later, I took most of the flowers to the cemetery, spending hours making your plot look perfect. As I planted them in the ground, I couldn't help but wish you could enjoy their beauty year-round. I saved a few to dry out for your mom and brothers to put on your grave once your stone was placed.

The headstone became another point of contention. Initially, I had planned on an elaborate lion-sculpted headstone, as per your boys' request, costing around $8,000. However, given the turn of events, I opted for a simpler design to be placed next to Grandma Barbara, reducing the cost to less than $3300. In my heart, I knew you wouldn't have cared about the cost or grandeur of the stone. You were a simple man, after all. I made a promise to myself that day – in my will, I'd arrange for a double headstone with lions for both of us, where our ashes could be combined. I think you would have preferred that idea.

Shortly after returning from San Diego, I underwent surgery to fix my ruptured breast implants. The procedure was more complicated than before, as I had waited too long due to all the chaos. Dr. Laurence did an excellent job, and I made a mental note to trust only him for any future procedures.

Returning to work proved to be another challenge. The hospital's administrative oversight in submitting the necessary paperwork delayed my return, and I had to involve my psychiatric doctor to write a note allowing me to go back. Finally, on August 19, 2024, I stepped back into the familiar routine of work, grateful for the semblance of normalcy it brought to my life.

As I focused on finishing this book and restoring my life, I had to deal with practical matters, too. Selling the Infinity car I bought for Teagan, dealing with recall issues that couldn't be addressed until September 11, 2024, and deciding what to do with the music equipment Carter left behind served as constant reminders of the fractured relationships with your sons.

But amidst all this, a gnawing doubt about the circumstances of your death began to consume me. The more I thought about it, the more holes I found in the story of your supposed suicide. The only witness was Carter, and after everything that had transpired, I found it hard to trust his account.

The gun used wasn't yours – it belonged to Mary Jane, a friend of Sage Terry. Her story about how you acquired the gun changed, raising red flags. Why would you use someone else's gun when you had your own in your backpack? Why didn't the police investigate Mary Jane more thoroughly?

As your mom and I pieced together the events of your last day, more inconsistencies emerged. Carter claimed he asked you to leave because you were drunk, but we found out there was a party at the house that night with drinking and drugs involved. Why single you out when everyone was drinking?

Your text message to Carter asking if everything was okay in the house didn't make sense either. You had spent Saturday night and Sunday morning there fixing his electricity. Why would you need to ask if everything was okay unless something had happened that forced you to leave?

The official story – that you went to a neighboring town bar, were driven back to the house at 1 a.m., had an argument with Casey, were kicked out by Carter, and then supposedly shot yourself right outside – felt fabricated. The police didn't question anyone else, didn't check for security camera footage from neighbors, and didn't even take fingerprints from the gun.

Even more disturbing was the information from the police scanner. Demonte had referred to you as *"Sutton Harris"* when talking to the police despite knowing your real name was Harrington. He claimed you were his neighbor, even though he knew you were visiting to help Carter with the electricity. These lies only deepened my suspicions. The more I dug, the more convinced I became that you didn't kill yourself. The inconsistencies in Demonte's statement to the police and the lack of thorough investigation all pointed to something more sinister. I made a vow then and there – I would not rest until this investigation was reopened. Even if it's the last thing I do, I will find the justice you deserve. You were my better half, my soulmate, and I know in my heart that this was not a suicide. Your mom and brothers share this belief, and we will not stop until we uncover the truth.

As I sit here, writing these words, I feel a mix of grief, anger, and determination. The path ahead is unclear, but I know I must walk it. For you, for the truth, for justice. I pray every day for God's guidance, for a path to the truth to reveal itself. Sometimes, in my darkest moments, I even hope to join you in heaven soon, but I know I have work to do here first.

The celebration of your life may be over, but the fight for justice has just begun. I will dedicate all my time and energy to finding the real story behind your death. The truth will eventually come out – I have to believe that. And when it does, I hope it will bring some measure of peace, not just to me but to all who loved you.

In the meantime, I'll continue to visit your grave, tend to the flowers, and talk to you as if you're still here. Because, in many ways, you are. Your spirit lives on in my heart, as do the memories we shared and the love that continues to bind us together.

As I close this book, both literally and figuratively, I'm reminded of something you once told me: *"The truth always finds a way."* I'm holding onto those words now more than ever. Whatever it takes, however long it takes, I will find the truth about what happened to you that night. And in doing so, I hope to honor your memory and bring you the peace you deserve.

Rest easy, my love. I'm on the case and won't give up until justice is served. That's a promise. While I've put your body to rest, I won't rest until I've uncovered the truth and found the justice you deserve. As I close this book, I open a new chapter in my life - one dedicated to uncovering the truth and ensuring that your story doesn't end here. Your memory will live on in these pages and every step I take toward justice.

Steve and Julia

www.ingramcontent.com/pod-product-compliance
Lightning Source LLC
LaVergne TN
LVHW050546160826
845677LV00011B/2196

9798230614869